THE HISTORY OF
MUSICAL
INSTRUMENTS
and Music-Making

THE HISTORY OF
MUSICAL
INSTRUMENTS
and Music-Making

A complete history of musical forms and the orchestra

MAX WADE-MATTHEWS

southwater

This edition is published by Southwater, an imprint of Anness Publishing Ltd, Hermes House
88–89 Blackfriars Road, London SE1 8HA; tel. 020 7401 2077; fax 020 7633 9499

www.southwaterbooks.com; www.annesspublishing.com

Anness Publishing has a new picture agency outlet for images for publishing, promotions or advertising.
Please visit our website www.practicalpictures.com for more information.

UK agent: The Manning Partnership Ltd; tel. 01225 478444; fax 01225 478440; sales@manning-partnership.co.uk
UK distributor: Book Trade Services; tel. 0116 2759086; fax 0116 2759090;
uksales@booktradeservices.com; exportsales@booktradeservices.com
North American agent/distributor: National Book Network; tel. 301 459 3366; fax 301 429 5746; www.nbnbooks.com
Australian agent/distributor: Pan Macmillan Australia; tel. 1300 135 113; fax 1300 135 103; customer.service@macmillan.com.au
New Zealand agent/distributor: David Bateman Ltd; tel. (09) 415 7664; fax (09) 415 8892

Publisher: Joanna Lorenz
Managing Editor: Judith Simons
Project Editor: Felicity Forster
Editor: Beverley Jollands
Photographer: John Freeman
Designer: Ian Hunt
Cover Design: DW Design
Picture Researchers: Cathy Stastny and Daniela Marceddu
Cover Picture Credits: front – Art Archive Ltd (16th-century Italian virginalist with viola da gamba, lute and recorder);
back – AKG, London (early 19th-century Russian horn band)
Production Controller: Claire Rae

ETHICAL TRADING POLICY
Because of our ongoing ecological investment programme, you, as our customer, can have the pleasure and reassurance of knowing that a tree is being cultivated on your behalf to naturally replace the materials used to make the book you are holding. For further information about this scheme, go to www.annesspublishing.com/trees

Previously published as part of a larger volume, *The Illustrated Book of Musical Instruments*

PUBLISHER'S NOTE
Although the information in this book is believed to be accurate and true at the time of going to press, neither the authors nor the publisher can accept any legal responsibility or liability for any errors or omissions that may be made.

Contents

Introduction

Music is the universal language of mankind.

HENRY WADSWORTH LONGFELLOW (1807–82), "OUTRE-MER"

There are few people who do not react to music to some degree. The power of music is diverse and people respond in different ways. To some it is mainly an instinctive, exciting sound to which they dance or move their bodies. Other people listen for its message, or take an intellectual approach to its form and construction, appreciating its formal patterns or originality. Above all, however, there can be hardly anyone who is not moved by some kind of music. Music covers the whole gamut of emotions: it can make us feel happy or sad, nostalgic or energetic, and some music is capable of overtaking the mind until it is oblivious to all else. It works on the subconscious, creating or enhancing mood and unlocking deep memories.

ABOVE: *The Amati Quartet led by Attila Balogh was one of the foremost chamber ensembles of the 1980s and early '90s. This picture, taken in 1988, shows the quartet giving one of their recitals.*

Music is intimately bound up with important events in all our lives. There is hardly a ceremony, whether personal or national, that is not accompanied by music. It may be as simple as the nightly ritual of a mother singing her baby to sleep or as formal as the playing of a national anthem. It may be a spontaneous outpouring of mass emotion, such as the spectators singing before a football game, or it may be a highly wrought and carefully rehearsed performance of massed bands or choirs at a great state wedding or funeral.

The history of music is a part of the history of humanity. Ethnographic studies of ritual among primitive societies have provided plenty of evidence to show that music-making is a basic and universal instinct. Because it is not a concrete art form, we can have no knowledge of what music sounded like in the centuries before

ABOVE: *Instruments that were in use in the Iberian peninsula during the 13th century included a portative organ, cornetts, double bladder pipe, bagpipes, lutes and shawm.*

ABOVE: *A performance of* Carmen *at Blackpool Opera House in 1938. Bizet's most successful opera opened in Paris in 1875, during the last year of his short life.*

ABOVE: This painting by Anne Vallayer-Coster, entitled The Attributes of Music, *was completed in 1770, just before the French Revolution and the beginning of the Romantic period in music. The instruments (from left to right) are horn, cornemuse, lute, flute and violin.*

it began to be written down or, much later, recorded. But very early written accounts remain, as well as ancient instruments and pictures or carvings showing them in use, to convey some idea of the importance of music to ancient civilizations.

In the 20th century, there has been an unprecedented interest not only in the written remains of the music of previous generations, but in establishing how such music really sounded. As recently as the 18th century, musicians were expected to provide only new works for concert audiences, whereas modern music-lovers are avid for music from all historical periods, often performed on instruments and in styles that attempt to recreate the

effect intended by the composer. There are many ways in which we try to understand the lives of previous generations in order to set our own lives in a secure context, and music is a powerful way of evoking the past.

At the same time, musicians are constantly seeking new forms of expression. As in every other contemporary art form, originality is highly prized in music, and every new development in technology is explored by both composers and players. Recording techniques have made all forms of music instantly available to a universal audience, but have not diminished the demand for live performance, on a wider range of instruments than ever before.

ABOVE: At the far left of this 15th-century Spanish painting are three singers reading from sheet music, accompanied by a band of six musicians on the right.

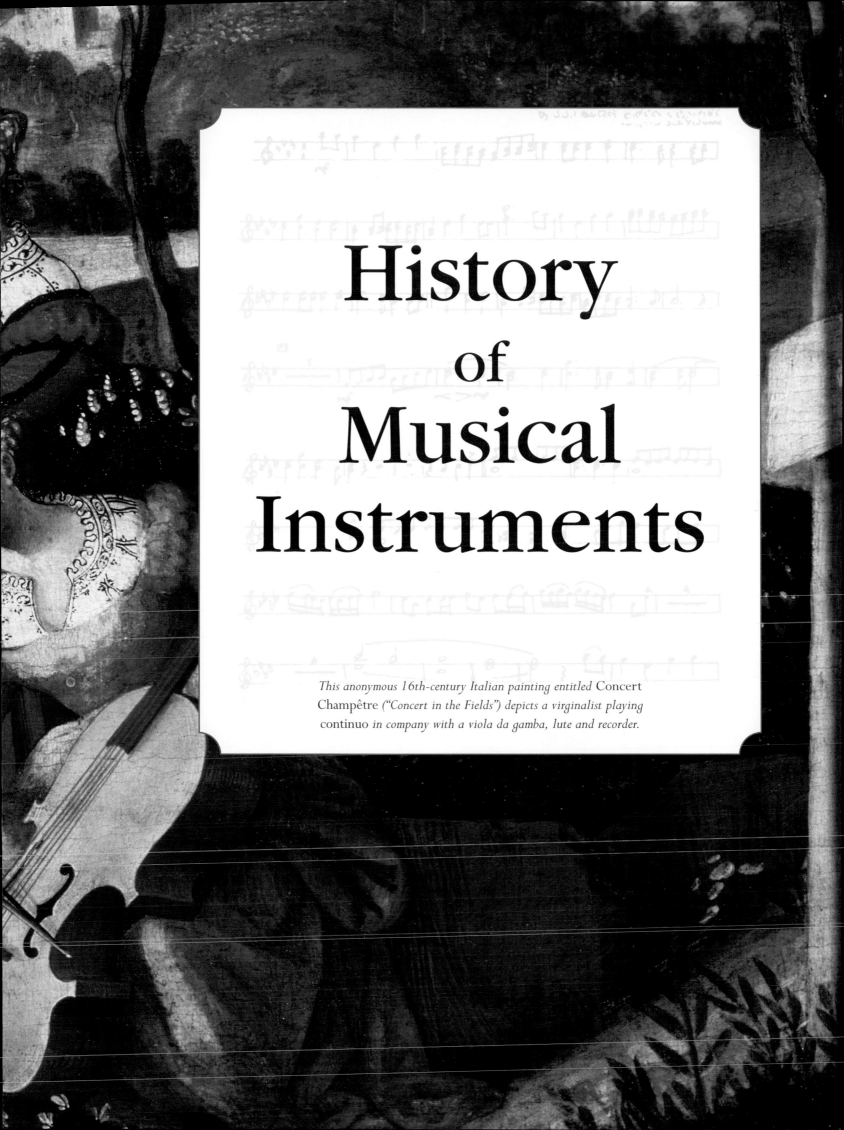

History
of
Musical
Instruments

This anonymous 16th-century Italian painting entitled Concert
Champêtre *("Concert in the Fields") depicts a virginalist playing*
continuo *in company with a viola da gamba, lute and recorder.*

What is Music?

Musick is a tonick to the saddened soul.

ROBERT BURTON (1577–1640), "ANATOMY OF MELANCHOLY"

When asked "What is music?" people will give various replies. Some will try to be scientific and say that music is a succession of sound waves. But that is also the result of scratching a blackboard with the fingernails, which most people would not describe as music.

The making of music is not restricted to human beings. Many animals, such as whales and birds, appear to use music as a means of communication. Natural music was utilized by the French composer, Olivier Messiaen, who used to go out into the countryside to transcribe birdsong, which he incorporated almost note-for-note into his orchestral and piano music. The American composer John Cage believed that the mechanical background sounds of everyday life could be described as music, and other composers have written works

ABOVE: Although birdsong is not created for a human audience, it is still music to human ears and one of the pleasures of life.

requiring all kinds of everyday objects to be used as "musical instruments".

Perhaps an easier question would be "What is not music?", though the answers would be just as varied. To some, the sounds made by a heavy metal rock band constitute music, while to others they are just highly amplified noise. Rock music of the 1950s and '60s, such as the songs of Buddy Holly, Jerry Lee Lewis, the Beatles or the Rolling Stones, was adored by its teenage fans but dismissed as unbearable noise by many of their parents. Many of Berlioz's contemporaries harked back to the "good old days" of Bach, while many early 20th-century music-lovers were none too impressed when confronted with the ground-breaking compositions of Stravinsky.

When André Previn was once asked the difference between popular and classical music, his reply was that there

was no such thing as popular or classical music, there was just good music and bad music. While there are many wonderful "classical" works, there are some that are not worth the manuscript paper upon which they were written. Conversely, as there are many popular songs that end up in the dustbin of history, there are many modern tunes that Mozart would have been proud to have written.

Beauty is in the ear, as well as the eye, of the beholder, and the

ABOVE: Drums are known to all cultures. This sculpture of a figure playing a small frame drum dates from AD 800, and is of the Peruvian Mochica culture.

ABOVE: The military drum was originally used as a means of signalling in battle, and was also beaten to set a rhythm that focused the minds of marching troops.

ABOVE: Rattles made out of gourds are one of the oldest percussion instruments and have been found in every part of the world.

Listening to music is a psychosomatic experience that, as well as promoting harmony and peace, holds a power for inner reassurance and satisfaction which stems from deep within the human spirit. Many people would

appreciation of a piece of music depends to some extent on the listener's culture and upbringing. To someone born in the West, for example, the music of East Asia is mysterious and possibly difficult to listen to, because its idiom is unfamiliar. However, once its context is understood and Western preconceptions about musical conventions are set aside, it becomes more accessible. Even without understanding, all music has the power to exert an effect on the emotions.

count themselves the poorer without it. We do not have to go into the science and philosophy of music to find the answer to our question; we simply need to go into our own souls, for that is where music belongs.

ABOVE: While the ringing of a single church bell might not be classified as music, a peal of three or more certainly is.

LEFT: The Portuguese Quineto de Cristal *in 1882. Crystallophones were a 19th-century innovation and for a while were very popular in Europe and the United States. The glasses were arranged in five octaves and struck with small hammers. In time interest flagged, and crystallophones became historical curiosities.*

What is a Musical Instrument?

Music is the sound of universal laws promulgated.

HENRY THOREAU (1817–62)

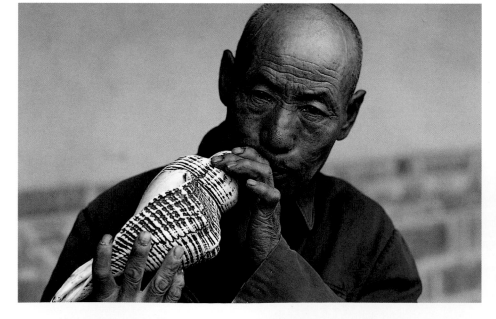

M usical instruments and their story have always been part of human history, and the story of music begins with the story of humanity. Music, or sound, stood at the cradle of all religions. When primitive humans struck a piece of rock, stone or skin, or blew into an old bone or hollow branch, they perhaps concluded that what they heard was the voice of the object. They therefore assumed that by awakening the "voice" of the object, they could propitiate the unseen nature of which their life was a part.

The rhythmic articulation of time by means of an instrument of some kind is far older than the construction of a true musical instrument. Any objects that early humans happened to pick up when singing or dancing could become sound-producing "musical instruments". Implements created for use exclusively as musical instruments developed only very slowly and many, if not all, early instruments (such as the pot drum) were merely adaptations

LEFT: Very early in human history it was found that a very loud sound could be produced by blowing into a conch shell.

of artefacts already invented for some other purpose. Instruments are the working tools of music; they are the practical devices by which the acoustic properties of nature are managed for the artistic purposes of music that begin with the player. The musical instrument cannot be separated from the musician. In the hands of an incompetent amateur, the finest Stradivari may as well be a block of wood. However, in the hands of a virtuoso, even a crude violin can sound heavenly.

Obviously, we do not know the world's first "tunes". The development of music predates the invention of writing by thousands of years, and there is no way of knowing what

ABOVE: The conch shell is still used as a musical instrument in present-day China; at some temples the shell is blown to announce the beginning of prayers. This conch shell has been fitted with a bamboo mouthpiece.

ABOVE: Rhythm plays an important part in African music. These painted wooden rattles are from Nigeria.

The two elements – the body and the column or box of air – together form a coupled acoustic system.

Other very early instruments include hollow tubes such as reeds and bones, and conch shells, which are believed to have been used as signal instruments. It is possible that these were at first shouted into, until it was discovered that more pleasing sounds could be produced by blowing.

sounds the Neanderthals and early *Homo sapiens* enjoyed. The first "instrument" was certainly the human voice, and ritual chanting is likely to have been accompanied by rhythmic clapping or stamping. This in turn would have led to the striking of an object, such as a convenient log or stone, which could produce a different, and probably a louder, sound.

These early musical instruments, made of naturally sonorous materials, are termed "idiophones". Modern percussion instruments, such as gongs, wood blocks, cymbals and xylophones, are also examples of idiophones. Before long the early musician would have realized that the sound produced by hitting a solid log was different from that produced by a hollow log. The latter is an example of the coupled system of sound production, in which the vibrations are excited in one source with the collaboration of an associated structure – such as the air in the log. This discovery is the foundation of the design of modern wind instruments, such as the horn or oboe, and of the body and soundbox of stringed instruments, such as the violin.

ABOVE: Scrapers are some of the earliest percussion instruments and are known virtually everywhere. These examples from Laos are made from bamboo.

RIGHT: Shakers or rattles come in various shapes and sizes, such as a plastic ball, metal box, wicker basket and natural pod.

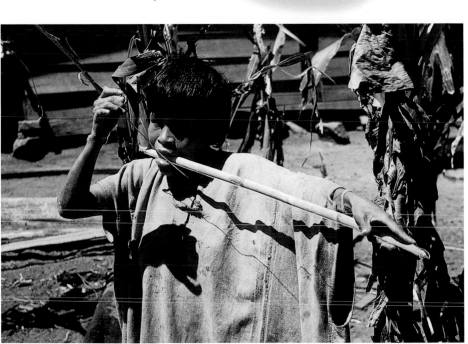

ABOVE: Musical bows are known almost all over the world. Often the mouth serves as a resonator while the string is set in vibration by either being tapped with a small stick, as in this example from Colombia, or plucked with a plectrum.

Music of Ancient Civilizations

*Provide me now a man that
can play well and bring him to me.*

1 SAMUEL 16:17

The earliest archaeological evidence of the use of musical instruments dates from about 3000 BC. By then, the Sumerians, an ancient society living in the fertile crescent of Mesopotamia, had assembled a range of musical instruments, including lyres, harps and reed-pipes, which may have been played as an ensemble. It is also known from written records that they practised antiphonal singing or chanting in their temples. There is no way of knowing what their music sounded like, but it is clear that it was a sophisticated part of Sumerian culture and that it had religious and ceremonial significance.

Egypt

The importance of music in ancient Egypt cannot be overestimated. Music was one of the concomitant joys of life; indeed, as a sign of this, the soundbox of the harp was sometimes fashioned to represent the sacred lotus flower in bloom.

ABOVE: This finely decorated 12th-century BC Egyptian harp is depicted on a tomb painting in Anhour Khaou's tomb in Thebes. In reality the left hand would have played the "back" of the instrument.

From the beginning of the New Kingdom in about 1550 BC, music, which was mainly performed by women, began to play a very prominent part in religious life. Many of the first musicians in the temples were the wives and daughters of priests, the more senior of whom enjoyed a high status second only to that of the king. The instrument of sacerdotal potency and ecclesiastical authority was the *sistrum*, a type of rattle with metal discs strung on a framework of wires, which symbolized divine power. Egyptian temple music was much more than just chanting and jingling. Harps, pandoras and pipes were also used to praise the gods, since it was part of the regular duties of the priest to extol the god in song, and dancing, accompanied by temple musicians, played an important part in many cults.

As time went on and the empire broadened, female slaves from captured nations were brought back to Egypt to serve as musicians. They attended academies of music where they were instructed in both singing and playing instruments. Music in Egypt was of such a high standard that even the Greeks commended it. Instrumental music was important in secular as well as religious life. Musicians played in homes as well as at feasts, in processions and at funeral ceremonies.

The earliest evidence of parallel pipes in Egypt is from about 2700 BC. Divergent pipes came into use – and in

ABOVE: A Theban tomb painting shows a musician playing double shawm pipes and another holding a lute-type instrument.

fact largely replaced the older instrument – in about 1500 BC. The divergent pipes were held with one pipe in each hand, with the proximal ends forming a V. Played exclusively by

ABOVE: This Egyptian wall painting dates from about the 15th century BC and shows a female musician playing an angular harp.

women, each pipe originally had four finger-holes, but later five or six became common. The right hand played the melody while the left pipe sounded a drone accompaniment.

The frame drum arrived in Egypt in about 1550 BC. Also played only by women, the drum accompanied many aspects of Egyptian life, ranging from the cult of Osiris to the dancing of the slaves in the Pharaonic court. Frame drums were similar in

ABOVE: *This Egyptian tomb painting from Thebes, 1425 BC, depicts dancers performing to the music of a double shawm.*

appearance to the modern tambourine, complete with jingling metal rings, discs or pellet bells.

Israel

In ancient Israel, music had a place in almost every activity and at almost every event. The double-headed drum, in the form of the *tof*, is known to have been played in Biblical times, when women used it to accompany their songs and dances. Until about 1000 BC music was the spontaneous outpouring of the people. Later, however, with the establishment of a trained and official body of musicians to lead worship in the temple, it became more formal and more ritualized. Trumpets represented the power of God, and the cantillation of scripture was a potent reminder of the sanctity of God's word, setting it apart from the unsanctified conversation of daily life.

Pipes were also known in Biblical Israel where smaller pipes, called *halil*, were made of cane or metal. The Hebrew prophets plied their trade under the influence of music and were

ABOVE: *A Hebrew coin dating from about AD 135 depicting a lyre.*

often preceded by musicians playing drums, pipes and lyres. (The Latin word *praecinere*, which was used in translations of the scriptures to describe their activity, means both to prophesy and to play the pipes.)

By 200 BC the temple had an established choir of 12 men and a number of boys, who sang to the accompaniment of lyres, pipes and cymbals. Antiphonal singing, which had been a part of Sumerian religious practice and was known to the Egyptians, was adopted by the Jews for the singing of psalms.

ABOVE: *An impression of the Temple of Jerusalem, used as an illustration to a 1732 Bible, showing Solomon dedicating the Temple to the Lord. Music was a feature of the Temple life, and trained musicians were employed to lead the worship.*

ABOVE: *One of the oldest horns still used today is the Jewish shofar. They are made from a billy goat's horn or a ram's horn.*

Classical Greece

That classical Greece was a musical Greece can be seen from the many modern musical words that owe their roots to Greek. Apart from "music" itself, they include "melody", "harmony", "symphony", "orchestra", "organ", "chorus" and "rhythm". The Greek work *mousike* embraced not only what is considered to be music today but also the text and accompanying dance. Greek poets did not just write the words, they also produced the work, trained the singers and dancers (who were mainly amateurs) and directed the accompaniment.

To the Greeks, music, singing and dancing were the main characteristics of a civilized society. They used music for many different purposes, ranging from celebration and the worship of gods to the boosting of morale. Musicians played to workers performing repetitive jobs, such as spinning and weaving, rope-making, grinding corn and treading grapes.

Music also played an important role in military exploits. An essential member of an Athenian trireme's crew was the aulete, or double-pipe player, who played to keep the rowers in time. Spartan armies marched to the sound of the aulos, which kept them at a steady pace without breaking rank. Aulos music also served as a morale booster to the troops, in much the same way as Scottish Highland regiments use the bagpipes today.

Greek contests

The notion of competition was dear to the hearts of the Greeks, and music was no exception. As a focus for competition, the art of *kitharodia* (singing to the self-accompanying of a kithara, or lyre) dates from about 670 BC. Choral contests were instituted about 50 years later, while in 580 BC the Spartans introduced aulos music into their public contests. These festivals were a magnet for performers, who came from great distances to take part.

Kithara versus aulos

During the 5th century BC, musical styles changed radically, as traditions were ousted by new ideas. Plato (c.428–347 BC), who was suspicious of change and denounced the new style as entertaining rather than edifying, complained about the "modern music" of his day, especially the use of the versatile aulos in preference to the kithara, which had also been adapted in an attempt to imitate the aulos and now had an expanded number of strings. Such was Plato's aversion to the aulos that he banned it from his ideal republic, believing that those who could not play the kithara were lacking in education.

Ancient Rome

Music was a rich and constant presence in Roman life. The everyday life of the Romans abounded in songs concerned with all subjects, ranging from reaping to weaving, from weddings to funerals and from love to satire. In the homes of the wealthy, music was often played during dinner, while in the theatre, plays and comedies often included the music of the *tibia* (the Roman version of the aulos) or the hydraulis, or water-pipe. The hydraulis also had a place in the arena, where it was often played with brass instruments, such as the *cornu* and *tuba*, to accompany chariot fights and gladiatorial contests

ABOVE: That music played an important part in Greek cultural life can be seen from this 5th-century BC vase painting depicting a young man learning to play the lyre.

ABOVE: The Roman Colosseum, seen here as it was in 1835, was a centre of Roman entertainment, much of which was to the accompaniment of music.

ABOVE: This Etruscan wall painting of the early 5th century BC shows an ambulatory musician playing an aulos, or double pipe. The player was known as an aulete.

in the arena. Pantomimes, another popular Roman entertainment, regularly incorporated choral singing, instrumental music and dancing.

Cult music in Roman life ranged from elaborate festival performances to accompaniments for the ritual slaughtering of an animal, when the playing of the *tibia* drowned out the cries of the doomed creature. Roman professional musicians had their own associations, which furnished performers for both public and private entertainments: extravagant fees were not unknown for the more popular musicians. Because of their connection with the state cult, these musicians benefited from certain privileges, such as being allowed to roam the streets unhindered, even though they were masked and frequently drunk.

ABOVE: Second-century Roman mosaic of a hydraulis, the ancestor of the modern organ. Under the pipes was a keyboard that operated perforated sliders. When a key was pressed, a slider was pushed into position to release pressurized air from the wind canal and thereby sound the note. The scene also shows a cornicin, a large and powerful circular horn.

ABOVE: First-century BC relief from Denmark depicting Celtic carnyx players. These instruments have a warlike appearance with their bells shaped like grotesque boars' heads.

India

The origin of the classical music of northern India is shrouded in obscurity. It is a mixture of many ancient cultural influences and the result of a long process of integration of various types of music that makes it one of the world's greatest art forms. The Sanskrit hymns of the *Rig Veda*, composed between the 14th and 10th centuries BC, were – and still are – intoned, and it is possible that the style that is used today has survived virtually unchanged from the time of their composition.

Hindus believe in the power of *samgita*, which encompasses vocal music, instrumental music and dance, to influence the universe and to play a part in freeing the individual from the cycle of birth, death and rebirth.

Raga

The *raag* is the mainstay of northern Indian classical music. There are some 200 main *raga*, each with its own scale pattern and specific rules. Some are linked with specific seasons and times of day, while some are feminine and others masculine.

The performance of a *raag* always follows a set pattern. It begins with the

ABOVE: This painting of Indian marriage celebrations in 1561 shows guests dancing to the rhythm of tambourines, tabla drums, trumpets and cymbals.

ABOVE: This 17th-century painting from India depicts lotus-flower dancers performing to the music of a dhola *drum and sitar.*

alapa, a slow, meditative mood-setter that introduces the notes of the scale in free time and is unaccompanied by drums. This can last several hours, although more usually it is a matter of minutes. The next two sections are the *jorh* and the *jhala*, in which the soloist begins to introduce a rhythmic element and explore complex variations.

The final section, the *gath*, introduces the tabla, a set of two drums played with fingertips and palms. The right-hand drum is the *tabla* and the left-hand one the *bayan*.

Both drum heads are made of skin with a paste of flour and iron filings in the centre. The *tabla* body is made of wood and that of the *bayan* of metal.

Qawwali

Another type of music associated with northern India (and Pakistan) is *qawwali*, a spiritual song that is intended to transport the mystic towards union with the creator. *Qawwali* music can be traced back at least as far as the 9th century, and in its present form to the late 13th century.

A feature of modern *qawwali* is the harmonium, an instrument introduced to India by Christian missionaries around AD 1900. Although the harmonium has the advantage that it does not need constant retuning, it does not meet with universal approval and is banned from All Indian Radio because it does not conform to the traditional flexible intonation of *sruti* music, in which the "same" note can acquire different, but recognizable, pitches in ascent and descent. Neither can the glides and swings of *gamaka*

ABOVE: *The young Indian prince Shri Raga listens to the music of the vina, an instrument characterized by a long string carrier and gourd resonator.*

ABOVE: *This Indian scene depicts the celebrations during the birth of Timur. The musicians are playing instruments such as cymbals, tabla drums and trumpets.*

music be achieved on the harmonium. The celebrated musician Rabindranath Tagore once went as far as to call the harmonium "the bane of Indian music".

Indonesia

The most famous music of South-east Asia is the vibrant, thunderous gamelan, the percussion orchestra, consisting of gong-chimes, metallophones and gongs, which is played in Java and Bali. The tradition goes back well over a thousand years and is believed to predate the Hindu-Buddhist kingdom that was founded in Bali in the 7th century, when the Balinese arrived from Java, having been ousted by the arrival of Islam.

In no other country is music such an integral part of the daily life of the community. There is a greater concentration of orchestras in Bali than

anywhere else in the world. Here, however, as in the rest of the Indonesian archipelago, music does not have a particular religious significance, as it does for Hindus in India.

Spanning over five octaves, gamelan music is like a tree, with some instruments representing the trunk, some the branches and some the flowers. The various instruments of the gamelan include drums, bamboo flutes, cymbals, the *rebab* (an upright fiddle), the great gong, which can be up to 1m/3ft in diameter, and the *trompong* (a row of ten gong chimes set in a wooden frame). One group plays the core melody, while another group stresses this at regular intervals, generally one note in four. A third group expands the core melody with a range of up to three octaves, while a fourth doubles the melody an octave above. As well as these groups, various gongs provide punctuation and drums conduct the rhythmic undercurrent.

Javanese gamelan music is courtly and gentle; the players use padded mallets and the tempo is slow and serene. In Bali, the style is much brighter, louder and more exuberant, using wood or horn hammers and employing a greater dynamic range.

ABOVE: *Balinese gamelan percussion orchestras go back well over a thousand years.* Trompong *players are shown here, with tuned gongs in the background.*

Japan

Japanese musical history can be divided into several stages of development. The first stage is the period up to the 6th century when the country, which had previously been ruled by a number of clans, was developing into an imperial state. Shinto became the state religion, and the music and dance associated with it became the main body of court music. The second stage, which lasted for the next three centuries, saw the introduction of continental Asian music and dance, as well as Buddhism. It was during this time that *gagaku* came into being.

Gagaku court music is the oldest surviving music in Japan and has been preserved at the imperial court and at a few temples. Nearly 20 different types of instrument are used in *gagaku*, including the *sho* (a reed-pipe mouth organ), flute, drums, gongs and chimes. The various types of *gagaku* include *kangan* (instrumental ensembles), *bagaku* (dance music) and the ritual music for Shinto ceremonies.

ABOVE: The shakuhachi, *a bamboo end-blown flute with five finger-holes. The instrument originated in China and was taken to Japan by Buddhist priests in AD 935.*

ABOVE: Japanese girls playing a samisen *(a guitar-like instrument with three strings) and a* koto *(a 13-stringed zither).*

The third stage in the development of Japanese music came in the period between 900 and 1573. It was then that the theatrical form called *noh* was developed. A marriage of drama, theatre, music and dance, the beauty of *noh* lies in its refined symbolism and sophistication.

The last period saw the Japanese version of the zither, the *koto*, come into fashion. The *koto*, which has 13 silk strings that pass over movable bridges, is played mainly by women, who wear three long ivory plectra on the right hand: one on the thumb, one on the index finger and the third on the middle finger. The left hand is used to dampen the strings and change the pitch. Other Japanese classical instruments of the period include the *shakuhachi* (bamboo flute) and the *biwa* (lute).

Korea

The music of Korea can be traced back over 5000 years and is based on two modes, the *p'yongjo* (common in court music, such as *aak*, and folk songs) and the more widely used *kyemyonjo*. The greatest period of musical development in Korea was during the reign of King Sejong (1418–50). Not only did Sejong reputedly devise the Korean alphabet,

ABOVE: A Korean musician playing the koto, *a kind of zither.*

ABOVE: A Korean musician playing the soduang, *a two-stringed instrument with a round resonating box covered with leather at one end and open at the other to admit the neck.*

spectacular shapes as the dancers move their heads.

Korea is also known for large orchestras of flutes, oboes and bronze and stone chimes that still play on the first Sunday in May at the ancestral shrine in Seoul. This is a very colourful sight: the massive frames of the chimes are richly decorated with dragons and birds, and contrast with the bold, bright costumes of the musicians.

The *kayagum*, a 12-stringed zither, provides the accompaniment to vocal music and is also played as a solo instrument accompanied by the *changgo* (an hourglass-shaped drum) and the *taegum* (a wooden flute). It has been said that the beauty of *kayagum* music is that when a melody makes a leap down it sounds like a waterfall, and when it reaches the bottom the note vibrates in the same way that water bubbles at the foot of a waterfall.

but he also created an advanced system of musical notation.

Korea treasures its musical heritage, and classical Korean music is actively promoted at the Seoul National Classical Music Institute, where leading musicians are classed as national treasures.

The Korean tradition of *samulnori* drumming goes back at least a thousand years. Played by a quartet of musicians on drums and gongs, *samulnori* originated in the rural farmers' dances that are still performed by dancers wearing hats with long ribbons that swirl into

ABOVE: A Korean cholgo, *or temple drum, resting on a wooden stand shaped like a tortoise. In ancient mythology the world was deemed to rest on a tortoise.*

ABOVE: A Korean honga *orchestra playing Confucian ritual music. A feature of the orchestra is the* pyongyong *or stone chimes. Sixteen tuned stones are freely suspended in a wooden frame in two rows and are struck with a mallet made of cow horn; they continue to emit a clear sound for several minutes.*

Structuring Music

Music is the reaching out towards the utmost realities by means of ordered sound.

RALPH VAUGHAN WILLIAMS (1872–1958)

The Greek mathematician Pythagoras (c.570–500 BC) carried out the earliest known acoustical experiments. Knowing that the shorter the length of a string the higher the pitch will be, Pythagoras demonstrated that pleasing intervals were sounded when a string is divided into certain ratios. When the length is halved, an octave is formed; when it is reduced to two-thirds the pitch is raised by a perfect fifth; when reduced to three-quarters it gives the perfect fourth. The same applies to the length of a column of air in a wind instrument. Over the years the remaining intervals of the scale were filled in with tones and semitones and thus began the gradual progress that culminated in the recognition of

ABOVE: The number of lines in each staff varied. This music from the Furtmeyer Missal, *written for the Archbishop of Salzburg in 1481, is on a four-line staff.*

made thicker than treble ones – if they were all of the same thickness the lowest string in a piano would have to be about 6.5m/7 yards long.

Notation

The staff originated in medieval Europe as a means of recording plainsong. At first it was a single line around which the neumes, like small ticks, were placed to show the approximate melodic and rhythmic shape. Additional lines were added in the 11th century and the spaces, as well as the lines, were used to position the notes. By the 16th century, today's exactitude of recording pitch was arrived at when a pair of five-line staves became the norm, arranged as a "grand staff" with the top five lines

ABOVE: The frontispiece of Franchino Gaffari's Theorica Musicæ *(1492) showing Pythagoras playing instruments such as tuned bells, musical glasses and pipes.*

tonality, or key. This concept has since remained the basis of musical composition in the West, though smaller intervals, called "microtones", occur in other musical cultures, such as in Indian music, and have been used by some experimental composers of the 20th century.

Harmonic vibrations

It was not until the 17th century that the relationship between the frequency of vibration and the length, diameter, tension and density of the string was established. It was Galileo (1564–1642) who discovered that if either the string's thickness or length is doubled, the frequency of vibration, and consequently the pitch, is halved. For this reason, bass strings can be

ABOVE: This 12th-century plainchant from the Missale Romanum *shows the neumatic notation of the day. There is only one line of "notes" which rise and fall.*

ABOVE: This manuscript, entitled Sumer is Icumen In *(c.1240), uses a six-line staff.*

forming the treble clef and the bottom five lines the bass clef.

The *flat* sign, which originally applied only to the B line, originated as a lower case *b*. The natural sign was a square gothic *b* that was later modified to give today's symbol. The *sharp* sign originated as a cancelled *b* with a stroke through it.

Tonic solfa

The tonic solfa had its roots in the 11th century when a monk named Guido d'Arezzo devised a way to help singers learn a new melody by relating its notes to the pitches of certain syllables associated with a well-known tune. The tune he chose was a Latin hymn in which the first syllables of the first six lines were each set one note higher than the previous one. Using the first syllable of each line as his model, he came up with Ut, Re, Mi, Fa, So, La. Apart from the change of Ut to Doh and the addition of Ti, these syllables are still used today.

ABOVE: Guido d'Arezzo (991–after 1033), seen here on the left, is remembered for his development of a system of precise pitch notation through lines and spaces as well as for propagating the method of sight-singing that has evolved into the tonic solfa.

Strings

*There's not a string attuned to mirth
but has its chord in melancholy.*

THOMAS HOOD (1799–1845)

If we believe Greek legend, it was the twang of a bowstring that first made the god Apollo aware of the musical properties of a vibrating string. The fundamental pitch at which a stretched string, held in tension between two points, is heard, depends upon its length, thickness, weight and tension, together with the properties of the soundbox or soundboard. The frequency at which a given string will vibrate is inversely proportional to its length, proportional to the square of its tension and inversely proportional to the square of its mass, while the amplitude varies with the energy imparted and transmitted.

Materials

A string for a musical instrument may be made of any material that can produce a musical sound when it is held under tension and plucked, bowed or struck. Although most early

ABOVE: *These two putti, one playing a small harp and the other the portative organ, are from the frieze of musical angels in the Chapel of Isotta degli Atti in Rimini.*

strings were made out of gut or silk, many other materials have also been used, such as gold wire strings found in Persia dating from the 5th century BC. More recently, nylon or steel strings have become common, and many strings are bound with fine wire.

Gut strings were made from the guts of lambs, from seven to eight months old. After cleansing and pickling in an alkaline solution, the guts were twisted together under tension before being polished with pads made of hair. The final diameter of the string was determined by the number of guts used, which ranged from two for the smallest mandolin string, up to 120 for a double bass.

Methods of string-playing

There are three ways to excite the string: plucking, bowing or striking. Although plucking excites an active range of high harmonics, they are short-lived. Plucking imparts energy by a single impulse and there is no means of maintaining the vibration. The optimum place to pluck a string is about one-seventh of its length from the end, as this will give the best selection of harmonics as well as amplitude. If the string is plucked either with the fingernails or with a plectrum, it is displaced at a sharp angle and a bright sound is produced, as opposed to the duller sound made when it is plucked with the pad of the finger or thumb.

ABOVE: *A mid 13th-century fiddler playing with a large arched bow. The stick extends beyond the end of the hair, the projection serving as a handle.*

ABOVE: *This 13th-century illustration of King David shows him playing a harp whose arching neck terminates in an open-mouthed zoomorphic head.*

A more solid sound is obtained by striking the string (as on a piano or a dulcimer). A struck string vibrates longer, giving a slower decay in the upper harmonics. However, in the stiffer and tenser lower strings of the piano the vibrations tend not to subdivide indefinitely into the shorter lengths, causing the upper harmonics to be weaker, with most of the energy going into the lower harmonics. Like the plucked string, the struck string has only a single impulse for each note sounded.

One of the more pleasing sounds achieved from a string is by using a bow, which maintains the supply of energy for vibration and thus permits the playing of sustained notes. The sound depends on the position of the bow and the width of the hair brought into operation. Different sounds can be produced by bowing slowly with the full width of the hair, bowing near the centre of the string, bowing swiftly with the edge of the hair, or bowing near the end of the string.

Types of string

TOP ROW, FROM LEFT TO RIGHT: Until the 1970s many violinists used gut strings exclusively, but as the high-tensioned E string had a tendency to break easily, it was replaced by wire.

Viola strings are usually made of gut. The lower two, or sometimes all, are wire-wound.

Harp strings are like piano strings, except that they are plucked.

Most classical guitar strings are made of nylon. They are usually sounded with the left side of the fingernails, but some players prefer to use the right side of their nails.

BOTTOM ROW, FROM LEFT TO RIGHT: Acoustic guitar strings can be made of gut or steel, played with fingers or plectrum.

Mandolin strings are laid in four courses of two. Tuned to the same pitch as the violin, the strings are played with a plectrum.

The strings of the sitar are carried over two bridges, first the "small" bridge and then the "main" bridge. Tuning is achieved by the pegs, and beads are used for fine tuning.

The strings of a piano range in thickness from very thin top strings to the thickly wound bass strings shown here.

Bows

The Devil rides upon a fiddlestick.

WILLIAM SHAKESPEARE (1564–1616), "HENRY IV PART 1"

The use of a bow as an instrumental accessory originated in the Byzantine Empire but, because of the weak tone of early bowed instruments compared with that of plucked ones, it was considered to be worthy only of the "common people". It was introduced into Europe in the 11th century by the Islamic conquerors of Spain, and within 100 years the bow had become known and was being used over most of western Europe.

Early bows

The form of the early bows, which were in the shape of fully drawn hunting bows, differed greatly from those in use today. As its name suggests, the bow originally had a convex shape, designed to hold a band of horsehair under tension so that it could be drawn across the strings of an instrument to set up a sustained vibration. In time the bowed shape became longer and more slender,

ABOVE: Detail from Bellini's Maria with Child and Saints *(1505) showing an angel playing a large viol with a bow that shows the trend for the arch to become lower.*

ABOVE: Early bows, as the name implies, were similar in appearance to bows used in archery, with a high arched stick.

though it was still convex. By the 12th century, bows with a curve at one end – a type still occasionally found in eastern Europe – had become popular.

The horsehair was tied directly to the stick at both ends, and the player varied the tension while using the bow, to facilitate the playing of single strings or multiple stopping (drawing the string over more than one string simultaneously). To allow for this, the bow was held in the fist and pressure was exerted on the hair with the fingers.

Early bows differed greatly in size; they could be as small as 20cm/8in. In the 16th century, the violin was becoming a popular instrument for dance music, and short bows of about 35cm/14in were adequate for this purpose. Concert bows were substantially longer, and some were more than twice the

size of the instrument being played. Some bows had sticks that extended well beyond the end of the hair, the projection serving as a handle.

Modern bow

In the second half of the 18th century the bow underwent a number of radical changes, principally to suit the development of the violin as a solo, virtuoso instrument. The new designs were the work of François Tourte (1747–1835) and Wilhelm Cramer (1745–99). Cramer designed a concave bow, which quickly led to the abandonment of the convex version. Tourte widened the ribbon of hair to about 1cm/½in, composed of 150–200 strands cut

ABOVE, FROM TOP TO BOTTOM: The ribbon of the modern violin bow is made of horsehair. The viola bow is similar to the violin bow but is slightly larger.

ABOVE: The standard length of the cello bow is about 68cm/27in.

ABOVE: The double bass bow is shorter and heavier than the cello bow, and can be held either from above or underneath.

ABOVE: *The insipid tone of early bowed instruments was due to the bow stick being weak. The player could not tighten the hair and so the strings could not be firmly gripped.*

from white horses' tails. He attached this to a strong, movable frog, so that the tension on the hair could be adjusted and set at the beginning of the performance. The bow could now be held lightly with the fingertips, instead of being grasped firmly in the whole hand. This allowed much greater flexibility and delicacy of playing style, which facilitated the rise of the great 18th and 19th-century violin virtuosi.

ABOVE: *This illustration of 1830 shows the "old" and "new" styles of bowing the violin.*

Bach bow

The Bach bow was created by Knud Vestergard of Viby, Denmark to play the Bach solo violin sonatas "precisely as written", and is associated with the violinist Telmányi. The bow has a very high arch, with as much as 10cm/4in separating the bow stick and the hair at the highest point. When playing on individual strings the bow hair can be tightened by a lever worked by the thumb. By loosening the hair the player is able to encompass all the strings, and thus sustain multiple stops continuously. The creation, however, succeeds in playing Bach's music only as imagined by the bow's 20th-century inventor – not as Bach intended or heard it.

Tourte also fixed the length of the violin bow at about 75cm/30in and the playing hair at about 65cm/25in. To make the stick he chose red Brazilian pernambuco wood for its combination of strength and lightness. These innovations in design established the form of the standard modern bow, which is sometimes referred to as the "Tourte bow".

ABOVE: *Early 14th-century fiddler playing with a high arched bow. The player is gripping the bow where the stick extends beyond the end of the hair.*

ABOVE: *The modern bow, as used by American violinist Isaac Stern (born 1920). Stern's playing – particularly of the Barber and Bruch concertos – has thrilled audiences for over 50 years.*

Reeds

There's music in the singing of a reed.

LORD BYRON (1788–1824)

The sound of a reed instrument is initiated by the vibration of the reed, which sets up the vibration of the air column in the tube of the instrument. Reed instruments fall into two main categories, according to the use of the reed: they are known as "bleating" and "free". The ancient Greek aulos was an early bleating reed-pipe and is known to date back to at least 2800 BC.

Reed preparation

In ancient Greece, cane for making aulos reeds was cut during early summer, when at its most elastic,

and laid out to season in the open. It was scraped and cleaned during the following spring, and cut into segments at the nodes: each internode furnished two reeds. Segments closer to the root were suitable for the left-hand pipe of the aulos and those closer to the tip of the stem were used for right-hand pipes. This is an indication that the left-hand pipe was the lower pitched of the two.

Today, reeds are still cut from the stem of the large semi-tropical grass *Arundo donax* or *Arundo sativa*, commonly, but inaccurately, called cane. The plants are specially cultivated in parts of Spain and southern France. They are now factory-cut, but many players learn to cut their own, a very skilled art. Various attempts to find substitutes for *Arundo donax* have been made from time to time, and materials as diverse

ABOVE: A single reed.

as silver and whalebone have been tried, but have never been successful. A recent development has been the use of manmade fibres, although the general consensus is that artificial reeds sound coarser than those made from natural cane.

Bleating reeds

A reed that beats against a surface is known as a "bleating" reed, and instruments that work on this principle can also be subdivided according to whether they use single or double reeds. The single reed, typified by that

ABOVE: A selection of different types of single reeds (from top to bottom) — clarinet, alto saxophone, tenor saxophone and baritone saxophone.

ABOVE: A selection of oboe double reeds — two baroque, classical, classical oboe d'amore, modern oboe, modern oboe d'amore, two cor anglais and bass oboe.

ABOVE: *The idea for a reed instrument must have evolved from people finding that blowing on a blade of grass produced a sound. This engraving is from Bonanni's* Gabinetto Armonico *(1723).*

ABOVE: *The various stages in making a reed. Top – the cut cane. Middle – the cane is cut in half, split and the scrape is shaped. Bottom – the final stages in shaping, trademarking and packaging the reed.*

of the clarinet, is a narrow slip cut to length, flattened on the inner side, and on the other side scraped down to a feather edge at one end. It is fastened to the mouthpiece of the instrument and vibrates against it.

The double bleating reed, typified by that of the bassoon, is made up of two slips of "cane", hollowed out on the inside until quite thin and again scooped to a feather edge on the outside. The two slips are then bound together and mounted in a short metal tube, known as the "staple".

Free reeds

The free reed is found mainly in certain organ pipes and bellows-blown instruments such as the harmonium and accordion. It is also used in the harmonica (mouth organ) as well as in the traditional Chinese *sheng*. The pitch

of the reeds, which are fastened over slots cut into the metal frame, can be lowered by filing near the fixed end, or raised by filing near the free end. A major development in the history

of the accordion was the introduction by firms such as Höhner, founded in Trossingen in 1857, of high-tempered steel reeds, which helped to ensure the instrument's popularity.

LEFT: *Although most professional oboe players make their own reeds, the process takes time and skill, and ready-made reeds are available.*

History
of
Music-
making

The modern symphony orchestra consists of around 20 different musical instruments. These can be categorized into four main groups: strings, wind, percussion and keyboards.

Evolution of the Orchestra

Musicke is said to be the rejoycing of the heart:
Musicke comforteth the mynde and feareth the enimie.

JOHN FLORIO (1553–1625), "FIRST FRUTES"

The word "orchestra" comes from the Greek, and originally meant the place where the Greek chorus sang and danced. In the Roman theatre, this space was reserved for the seats of senators. Later it was applied to the stage itself. The term was revived in the late 17th century, and by the early 18th century it had been applied in France to the players themselves.

The roots of the modern orchestra go back to the 16th-century consorts employed in noble households, and to the groups of instrumentalists

ABOVE: *Fifteenth-century Italian fresco of an angel playing a sackbut — a standard instrument in civic bands at this time.*

ABOVE: *Five musical angels from a triptych by Hans Memling painted in about 1480. The instruments depicted are the psaltery, tromba marine, lute, sackbut and tenor shawm.*

especially assembled for important occasions such as royal weddings and funerals. During the 17th century the composition of orchestras varied from place to place: strings were preferred in Italy, France and England, whereas the German courts preferred brass ensembles.

Municipal consorts

Musicians were employed by European civic authorities from as early as the 13th century. The first town known to have availed itself of a regular musician was Brunswick, Germany, in 1227. Florence in Italy and Ypres in Belgium had civic musicians by 1291 and 1297 respectively. In Germany, town musicians were known as *Stadtpfeifer* (town pipers) and in England as waits.

The duties of these official musicians were many and varied, ranging from civic functions to church festivals and celebrations.

English waits

The word "wait" derives from either Anglo-Saxon *wacian* or Old High German *Wahta*, both meaning "watch" or "guard". In time the word began to be used for the shawm, the instrument played by the watch, which was generally dubbed the "wait pipe". Many English towns possessed waits at an early date, York (1272) and Norwich (1288) being among the first recorded. The musical part of the waits' duties grew and by the mid 14th century three waits were included in the Royal Band of Edward III. By the

15th century most towns employed waits, whose main function it was to attend the mayor on ceremonial occasions and, in some towns, to play in the streets at night.

Most bands of waits performed only in their local area, but some travelled farther afield. In 1589 Sir Francis Drake employed five Norwich waits, equipped with their shawms, trombone and recorder, to provide shipboard entertainment for his expedition to Lisbon – forming what must have been the first ship's band.

German Turmmusik

Although Germany had had *Stadtpfeifer* since the 13th century, in the 16th century a phenomenon known as *Turmmusik* (tower music) became common. This was music played from the church or town-hall tower. The repertory of these bands consisted in the main of harmonized chorales but also included occasional *Turmsonaten*, which were played by instruments such as cornetts, trombones and trumpets, in four or five-part harmony.

ABOVE: Detail from a mural The Nuremberg Town Band, *painted in about 1500 by Albrecht Dürer. Pictured are two trombones, two cornetts, two shawms and a drum. Later that century a greater variety of instruments was in use, including recorder, viol, fiddle, cornett, guitar, lute, bandora and bagpipes.*

ABOVE: A 15th-century consort consisting of musicians playing small kettledrums, fiddle, horn, triangle, lute and bagpipes.

Sixteenth-century consort

The main instrument of a medieval consort was the shawm, a double-reed woodwind instrument that was first used in western Asia for dance and ceremonial music, and was brought to Europe by returning crusaders in the 12th century. The forerunner of the oboe, it had a piercing, brilliant tone, which made it especially suited for playing outdoors. It was initially used in folk music, and much later in opera.

Like its eastern prototype, the eight-holed European shawm was made from a single, conically bored piece of hardwood, terminating in a bell.

By the beginning of the 16th century shawms were being used in consort, and several sizes were made. The type instrument was the seven-holed treble, which was about 66cm/26in long. The shrill-toned soprano shawm was tuned a fifth above the treble and was about 48cm/19in long. The alto shawm, tuned a fifth below the treble, was about 76cm/30in long. The tenor shawm, which was tuned a fifth below the alto, was 112cm/4ft long and had a long S-shaped staple on which the reed and pirouette were mounted.

The bass instrument, which was known as the "bombarde" due to its resemblance to the newly invented artillery piece, was tuned an octave below the tenor and was 1.8m/6ft long. It had two keys at the front and two at the rear. There was also a giant bass shawm of about 3m/10ft in length which when played was passed under the musician's arm with the bell resting on the floor behind him.

Baroque Orchestra (1600–1750)

*Handel's entertainments are calculated for the Quality only,
people of moderate fortunes cannot pretend to them.*

THE ENGLISHMAN'S JOURNAL, 1738

In the 17th century, instrumental music was still the privilege of the great aristocratic and royal households that had the means to employ full-time orchestras and composers. Indeed, the only way that a composer could earn a living was to be employed as a servant by some wealthy patron, either a leading church dignitary or a member of the aristocracy.

A feature of Baroque music was the *basso continuo*, or figured bass, and most music was written for strings and a harpsichord. The harpsichord shared the bass line with the cello, but also added chords that helped to thicken the harmonic texture.

Italy

One of the first orchestras resembling those of today was formed in 1607 by Claudio Monteverdi (1567–1643).

ABOVE: Jean-Baptiste Lully (1639–87) is seen here with the score of Armide et Renaud, *which he composed in 1686.*

Language

By the early 17th century Italian composers had begun to write expression marks into their music, which is why today Italian is still, by convention, the language of Western music. Indeed such was the influence of Italy that some 19th-century English musicians adopted Italian versions of their plain English names, believing – not without good reason – that this would impress their public. The composer John Cooper (c.1570–1627) became Giovanni Coprario, and the Irish tenor and friend of Mozart, Michael Kelly (1762–1826) called himself "Ochelli". Charles Dickens satirized this curious affectation in his story *The Dancing Academy*, in which the dancing master is a certain Signor Billsmethi.

Employed by the Duke of Mantua at one of the richest courts in Italy, Monteverdi was able to use a 40-strong band of strings, flutes, cornetts and trombones for his opera *Orfeo*. The fusion of brass and strings – as opposed to the earlier orchestration of strings and woodwind only – had been adopted by many bands in northern Italy, particularly that of St Mark's, Venice, where Monteverdi ended his career.

This was a period when opera flourished in Naples in the hands of Alessandro Scarlatti (1660–1725). However, in Italy instrumental music also began to be played in its own right, independently of opera, and the concerto came into being. Two of the foremost Italian composers of this form were Arcangelo Corelli (1653–1713) and Antonio Vivaldi (1675–1741). Both wrote *concerti grossi*, characterized by the interplay between a large and a small group of instruments.

France

The *Vingt-quatre Violons du Roi*, which confusingly sometimes numbered 25, was set up to provide music at the court of Louis XIII (1601–43). It served as a training ground for the most brilliant players in France, as well as establishing a stylized method of playing dance music. The band, which had the reputation of decorating and embellishing everything it played, played from memory and as a result some of its performances were nothing short of disastrous. However, when Jean-Baptiste Lully became Louis XIV's *Compositeur de la Musique Instrumentale* he set up his own band, the *Petits Violons*. This band, whose members were the first to wear a uniform and to use their bows in the same direction, was greatly admired and soon became a model for the rest of Europe.

Public concerts

Although music had been banned in England during the Commonwealth (1648–60), on his return from exile in France it was not surprising that Charles II was quick to introduce French music and customs to the English court. One of the Royal violinists was John Banister who, in 1672, started organizing musical performances at his home, which an invited audience would pay to hear.

At the beginning of the 18th century, public concerts as we know them today were still unknown, and musical performances were restricted to the homes of the nobility. However, as the standard of living gradually rose, so did the mercantile class, whose new opulence stimulated a desire for novelty in all forms of artistic expression, including music. It was, however, still music by the upper classes for the upper classes.

Some of the earliest public paid-entry concerts in France were the *Concerts Spirituels*, which began in 1725 in a hall in the Tuileries, Paris.

ABOVE: The Concert *(1690) by A. D. Gabbiani shows seven Modena court musicians playing violins, cello and harpsichord.*

These were primarily performances of sacred music, sung in Latin, which took place on holy days in the church calendar (when the opera was closed). The difference between these events and those organized by Banister in England was that whereas Banister's audience consisted solely of invited guests, there were no restrictions on admission to the Paris concerts.

ABOVE: In the middle of the 18th century the rich still employed musicians to perform in their homes. This painting shows a group of patrons listening to a singer accompanied by a chamber band consisting of a harpsichord, two violins, viola and cello.

ABOVE: Johann Sebastian Bach performing on a piano before his patron Frederick the Great in May 1747.

Classical Orchestra (1750–1830)

Orchestral music is one of the glories of the world.

GEORG SOLTI (1912–97)

The love of orchestral music had become so widespread by the year 1775 that it was said that even "common servants" could be met who pretended "as much judgement of an opera tune as my Lady Duchess". It was also a period when professional performers began to make large fortunes and composers were able to make an independent living, without having to tie themselves to any one court or church. Two of the first truly independent composers were Wolfgang Amadeus Mozart (1756–91) and Ludwig van Beethoven (1770–1827).

ABOVE: London's 18th-century Vauxhall Gardens were the centre of social intercourse for the upper classes. Anybody who was anybody spent time there chatting to the background music of the house band.

Instrumentation

Mozart wrote his early symphonies for the forces he had available, namely strings, two oboes and two horns. By 1782, however, he was independent and began writing for his ideal orchestra, which included flutes, clarinets, bassoons, trumpets and kettledrums. It was, however, Franz Joseph Haydn (1732–1809) and Beethoven who established the nucleus of the modern symphony orchestra; by 1800 the average size of the orchestra was about 40.

Mannheim

One of the first "modern" symphony orchestras was founded by Johann Stamitz (1717–57) at the court of Duke Karl Theodor at Mannheim, Germany, in 1742. The Mannheim orchestra consisted of 50 virtuoso players, making it the largest regular ensemble in Europe at that time. "Its *forte* was like thunder, its *crescendos* like mighty waterfalls, its *diminuendos* like a gentle river disappearing into the distance, its *pianos* like a breath of spring." When a long *crescendo* began it was not unknown for the audience gradually to rise from their seats. This *crescendo* became known as the "Mannheim Steamroller", while an expressive falling phrase was the

ABOVE: Mozart was one of the few musical child prodigies whose genius developed with maturity. By the age of two he was already discovering chords on the keyboard and, by the time he was five, was performing on and composing pieces for the instrument. As well as 18 masses, 21 concertos and 41 symphonies, Mozart also wrote 12 operas, two of the most popular being The Marriage of Figaro *and* The Magic Flute.

"Mannheim Sigh", and various interpolated woodwind trills and turns were "Mannheim Birdies".

Subscription concerts

By the end of the 18th century concerts were being held frequently. Although they were now public events rather than private parties held in the homes of the nobility, they remained an exclusive form of entertainment due to the high price of subscriptions, which had become established by 1760. By charging in advance in this way, promoters of concerts knew just what money was available and thus were able to hire the finest performers they could afford. It was not until the middle of the 19th century that there was a change from subscriptions to the selling of tickets at reasonable prices.

In the days of Mozart and Haydn the audience did not sit quietly as (in theory) they do today, but engaged

in many activities, including eating, drinking, chattering to their friends and falling asleep. It is said that Haydn wrote his Symphony No. 94, nicknamed the "Surprise", to wake them up.

Music festivals

A phenomenon unique to British society during the Classical period was the music festival. Lasting two or three days, these were held in many provincial towns in aid of local charities, drawing in the famous musical names of the day to give local people a chance to hear what London audiences were able to enjoy on a regular basis. The annual *Three Choirs* festival, held in Gloucester, Worcester and Hereford, was one of the first to be founded, in 1724. Leicester held two such festivals in 1771 and 1774 and, in July 1803, just over the border in Warwickshire, Nuneaton held a two-day event. In 1823 and 1825 York held two very successful festivals and, in 1826, under royal patronage, over £2400 (US$1485) was raised in Birmingham, a town that had been holding triennial festivals since the 1790s. The forward march of

ABOVE: The band of strings and horns at the San Beneto Teatro. The musicians are placed in two serried ranks at the side of the hall in Venice.

ABOVE: By the early 19th century renowned opera singers such as Giuseppe de Begnis were performing virtuoso parts full of technically difficult vocal pyrotechnics.

19th-century musical life in Britain continued in 1813 with the founding of the London Philharmonic Society, whose main aim was to perform the great orchestral works of the day.

ABOVE: Beethoven, who had received his early musical education from his father, became a professional musician at the age of 11. Over the next few years he took lessons from Mozart and Haydn. Soon his aristocratic patrons recognized the worth of his work and gave him financial support for the rest of his life.

Romantic Orchestra (1830–1910)

It is scarcely credible that a distinct Romantic school could be formed in music, which is in itself romantic.

ROBERT SCHUMANN (1810–56)

By the 1850s the orchestra was increasing in size, and by 1880 it was not unusual to see an ensemble of 100 or more instrumentalists. Composers were beginning to treat the orchestra as a homogeneous whole rather than as diverse sections, with an increasing awareness of the importance of internal balance.

One of the greatest Romantic composers was Richard Wagner (1813–83) who, unlike earlier composers, was not content simply to write for the instrumental forces already present in the orchestra. As well as introducing existing instruments to the orchestra, he even specified the making of new ones, such as the bass trumpet and the Wagner tubas for *The Ring*. Hector Berlioz (1803–69) was also an

ABOVE: *A scene from the première of Wagner's* Rienzi, *performed at the Dresden Hoftheater on October 20, 1842.*

ambitious composer, and in his *Requiem* he called for a chime of 16 timpani. Gustav Mahler (1860–1911) wrote on an equally grand scale, and his Eighth Symphony was written for a chorus of 500, as well as 350 children's voices, seven soloists and an augmented

orchestra – not for nothing was this work nicknamed the "Symphony of a Thousand".

On June 17, 1872 the largest orchestra ever formed took part in a concert at the World Peace Jubilee in Boston, Massachusetts. The orchestra of 1000 instrumentalists and choir of 20,000 voices were conducted by Johann Strauss the Younger, who was on a tour of the United States. Armed with a long illuminated baton and 100 assistant conductors, he led the band (as Strauss later recalled) in an "unholy racket" such as he had never before or since heard.

Larger orchestras meant higher overheads and, as many orchestras no longer had royal patronage, it was only through the efforts of the rich music-lovers who sponsored events that most orchestras survived. Bigger concert halls were built to accommodate the large paying audiences that were needed at concerts to make the orchestras viable.

Promenade concerts

The concept of the promenade concert originated in France, where successful concerts were mounted in Paris by Philippe Musard and Louis Antoine Jullien. The format was brought to Britain, and the first London promenade concert was held in December 1838. Unlike promenade concerts today, where the audience is static, those attending these early events literally did promenade, chatting to their friends as the concert progressed. Music was a secondary

ABOVE: *Richard Wagner, one of Europe's finest Romantic composers, is seen here conducting the* Siegfried Idyll *on the steps of his house as a surprise for his wife Cosima on the morning of her birthday in 1870.*

ABOVE: *The cover of the sheet music for the* Promenade Quadrille *showing the Covent Garden Orchestra in London, 1870.*

concern, as the audience used the opportunity to show off their fashions.

Orchestral tours

By the 1840s, large musical groups were beginning to tour, both nationally and internationally. This was mainly due to the advent of the railways, which were able to transport large numbers of people (and baggage) much faster than horse-drawn coaches. At last people in the provinces were able to see and hear what those in the capital cities had been enjoying for many years. This led to a resurgence of interest in music, and many towns throughout Europe formed their own amateur bands and choirs.

The music of preceding generations began to be revived. In contrast to the 18th century, when most of the music played was contemporary, during the 19th century the works of

RIGHT: *An illustration of an English orchestra from the early 19th century.*

dead composers, such as Beethoven, Mozart and Handel, found a place in almost every concert.

It was not only bands that were taking advantage of the better transportation; composers and soloists such as Franz Liszt (1811–86), Niccolò Paganini (1782–1840) and Felix Mendelssohn (1809–47) also began to make provincial tours, to the delight of those who were unable to travel to hear them play in the big cities.

ABOVE: *A scene from a performance of Wagner's* Tannhäuser *at the Bayreuth Festival of 1972.*

ABOVE: *An early 19th-century performance in London's Vauxhall Gardens. A feature of the band are the two black musicians — one with a tambourine and the other with a Turkish crescent. An important development during the 18th century was the adoption by European bands of "Turkish" or "Janissary" music. The instrumentation depended heavily on percussion, and a feature of these bands was that percussion instruments were usually played by young black men. Dressed in the most exotic manner, they performed incredible acrobatics as they played.*

Modern Symphony Orchestra

There are two golden rules for an orchestra:
start together and finish together.

THOMAS BEECHAM (1879–1961)

After World War I the cost of mounting such colossal works as Mahler's Eighth Symphony became prohibitive and composers turned their pens to smaller combinations. One such composer was William Walton (1902–83) whose *Façade* was greatly influenced by jazz, as was *The Rio Grande* by Constant Lambert (1905–51). The divide between "serious" music and jazz narrowed, with jazz idioms also coming to the fore in Walton's *Belshazzar's Feast*, in which the squeaking flute sounds like a slate pencil scraping on a hard stone wall. Another composer who used both new and old musical forms was Michael Tippett (1905–98), who

ABOVE: The modern symphony orchestra usually consists of over 90 players, requiring a large concert hall for its performances. The Philharmonia Orchestra is shown here performing at the Royal Festival Hall in London.

ABOVE: For maximum volume, modern composers may include a large choir and percussion section in their compositions. The Bournemouth Symphony Orchestra and Choir are seen here under the direction of Kees Bakels. Founded in 1893, this orchestra has become one of Britain's foremost provincial orchestras and has been conducted by many great maestros.

incorporated motifs from spirituals in *A Child of Our Time* and blues and boogie-woogie in *Songs for Dov*.

In the 1950s the idea developed among composers that each separate instrument should be distinctly audible playing its individual part, rather than hearing the orchestra as an entity, a single giant instrument. Players now had to work much harder than before to give richness or beauty of tone-colour to the music.

Conductorless orchestra

The post-revolutionary Pervyi Simfonicheskii Ansambl (First Symphonic Ensemble) was formed in the USSR in 1922. The unusual aspect of the orchestra was that, believing that in the ideal Marxist state all men are equal, its members felt that there was no need to be led by the dictatorial baton of a conductor; instead they were led by a committee. Although it was a partial success, the principal difficulty with the concept was in changing tempo. The orchestra survived for ten years and had to be disbanded only when the individual talents began to rebel against the rigid control under which they were expected to play.

New instrumental techniques

Twentieth-century orchestral practice provided composers with a vast range of techniques. One composer who developed a remarkable effect was the Spanish composer Roberto Gerhard (1896–1970), who devised the ethereal ringing tone produced by stroking the edge of a cymbal with a double bass bow. Another novel use of the orchestra was that produced by Pierre Boulez (born 1925) in *Don* from *Pli selon Pli*, where he used the orchestra not as families of woodwind, brass and strings, but as three groups of high, medium and low-voiced instruments, irrespective of their colour.

ABOVE: A modern symphony orchestra stands to acknowledge the audience's applause.

Some composers, although writing music for the instruments of a conventional orchestra, arranged the instruments in unusual combinations. In his *Music for Strings, Percussion and Celeste*, Béla Bartók (1881–1945) divided the strings into two chamber groups placed on either side of a piano, harp, celeste and percussion section.

Another composer who experimented with new effects was Claude Debussy (1862–1918). His symphonic sketch *La Mer*, composed in 1905, was finished while he was staying at the Grand Hotel at Eastbourne in England, overlooking the sea, and is a well-known example of his impressionistic approach to composition. Although Debussy used large forces for his orchestral works, it was less to enhance volume than to create colour in his music.

Other new orchestral effects have been created by the woodwind deliberately overblowing, brass players being instructed to whisper, shout or yell into their mouthpieces, and string players being asked to produce harsh, grating sounds by bowing between the bridge and the tailpiece of their instruments. Compositions like these are set to continue breaking all the rules well into the 21st century.

ABOVE: A large symphony orchestra accompanying a group of jazz soloists.

The tragedy in the interpetation of music of the past lies in the fact that it is confined to concert halls, congresses of musicology, or conservatory classes. Music needs air, sunlight and liberty to be alive.

Wanda Landowska (1877–1959)

It has recently become fashionable to perform music with an authentic orchestra, using the number and type of instruments that the composer would originally have intended. Players and scholars alike have investigated early music and instruments in an attempt to discover just what was played and on what instruments, how it sounded and how it was performed. Indeed, such is the current situation that a concert of early music is likely to attract a larger audience than one of modern music.

There are special problems confronting the performer of authentic music, and each of these must be considered before calling a performance truly "authentic". Design and colour cannot be separated. In the same way that an outline drawn by Raphael could not be coloured in with Cézanne's palette, a modern violinist will not play in the same manner as Corelli. Even if he is playing on a 300-year-old instrument, he still has to know how the music was intended to be played.

Although modern composers use instruments which, by name at least,

ABOVE: Authentic music performances can be a living history experience. In this case a Salzburg violinist is dressed in 18th-century costume to enhance the period effect.

would have been familiar to Haydn and Beethoven, the style of playing and the sounds produced are totally different. Orchestral sounds changed completely with the introduction of Boehm flutes, Triébert oboes, Klosé clarinets and Heckel bassoons, not to mention valved horns and electronic instruments.

Another factor to bear in mind is the size of the orchestra's string section in relation to the wind section. In the 18th century it was unusual for an orchestra to have more than eight violins, 12 being rare. By the time of Beethoven's death a violin section of 32 had become common. However, there was no relative increase in the woodwind section. It follows therefore

RIGHT: A modern group of musicians dressed in late 18th-century costume recreating an orchestra playing Mozart's Te Deum.

Johann Stein to tune Mozart's piano had a frequency of 422Hz – half a tone lower than modern pitch. From 1800–50 the pitch in France rose from 423 to 446Hz. In 1880 Steinways were tuning their pianos to 457Hz – a quarter-tone above the present pitch.

The first attempt to fix a standard was made in 1834, but had no success. In 1889 it was decided to stabilize the pitch at 435Hz and by international agreement in 1939 "concert pitch" was fixed at a frequency of 440Hz.

that a work by Mozart played by a modern orchestra will not sound like the sonorities Mozart heard – the wind being lost under a mountain of strings. Unless the orchestra plays with the correct numerical relationship between the strings and wind, as the composer understood it, the sound will never be "authentic".

Any instrument that is used over a period of time undergoes changes. These changes invariably alter the sound produced and, as composers score for instruments according to how they perceive the sound they make, so does the way they write for them. Elgar did not write for the horn in the same way that Beethoven or Purcell did.

Pitch

It is not only the instruments, but also the pitch that has altered. From 1762–89 the tuning-note (A) varied between frequencies of 377 and 428 cycles per second, or Hertz (from a minor third to half a tone below the modern standard). Apart from this variation, musicians in different regions tuned to different pitches at the same time. France preferred a low, Germany a middle and England a high pitch. The tuning fork used in 1780 by

Chamber Music

*Chamber music concerns itself as a world of sound
that has external boundaries but no internal ones.*

HANS WERNER HENZE (BORN 1926)

Originally, the term "chamber music" described intimate music for small groups of solo instruments performing in a drawing room before either a small audience or with no listeners at all. Chamber music differs from other orchestral music in that generally only a single instrument performs each part, whereas in an orchestra the parts are played by groups of instruments.

Although there had been a lot of small-scale ensemble music in the Middle Ages, the medieval court was a place of public exhibition, with very little opportunity for domestic music-making. However, with the rise of instrumental music and an increasing interest in amateur vocal and instrumental music-making in the 16th century, music began to play an important part in the homes of the well-to-do.

Many great houses maintained one or more professional musicians and in 17th-century Italy some princely establishments appointed musicians who had special responsibility for the performance and composition of chamber music. Monteverdi held such a post in the household of the Duke of Mantua, and his contemporaries in similar posts included Enrico di Foggia and Sigismondo d'India.

ABOVE: A painting by Max Buri (1868–1915) showing a group of German village musicians in about 1910.

Another development of the period was the tendency to arrange vocal music for instruments. From the mid 16th century consort music for viols flourished, with compositions being circulated in manuscript copies. Some were published by composers such as Michael East (c.1580–1648) and William Byrd (1543–1623), who issued their collections in 1610 and 1611 respectively. During the 16th and 17th centuries many consorts were formed, the music of which led to the invention of new dances such as the slow, stately pavan and the quicker galliard, as well as the musical forms of *ricercare* and *canzona*, which in turn led to the development of the 17th-century sonata and fugue.

In the 17th and 18th centuries chamber music was encouraged in Germany by the flourishing *collegium musicum*, in Italy by the spread of music academies and in England by the formation of music clubs.

Eighteenth-century chamber music began to include wind instruments, especially in France where music for

ABOVE: A Musical Evening *by Michel Ange (1680–1730). The painting shows a chamber ensemble (harpsichord, cello, violin and flute) performing to a group of friends.*

ABOVE: *One of the finest musicians of the 20th century, Yehudi Menuhin, with his sister Hephzibah and the French cellist Maurice Gendron.*

ABOVE: *This painting by Pieter Fabris shows a group of mid 18th-century chamber musicians playing in Lord Fortrose's apartment in Naples, Italy.*

various combinations of violin, flute, oboe, bassoon and harpsichord was first published. This flexible instrumentation, much of which included a fully written-out harpsichord part, as opposed to the *continuo* required hitherto, seems to have been a development prompted by publishers rather than composers.

In the homes of the nobility regular music evenings were held, at which small groups of musicians played for the family and their guests. Some of these groups were professional musicians who were sponsored by the family. One such ensemble was the Rasumovsky Quartet in Vienna, which was founded and paid for by Count Rasumovsky, the Russian ambassador to Vienna, who played second violin in the group. It was considered one of the best in Europe and even Beethoven wrote pieces especially for it.

New instrumentation
In early 20th-century France there was a proliferation of works for combinations unknown before 1900.

There was a concentration on the flute and the harp – uncommitted instruments that suited the impressionistic age. Examples include the enchanting *Introduction and Allegro* by Maurice Ravel (1875–1937) and Debussy's trio, Sonata for Flute, Viola and Harp.

Another French chamber composer who went in for unconventional instrumentation was Pierre Boulez, who scored *Le Marteau sans maître* for flute, viola, guitar, vibraphone or xylophone and percussion. Igor Stravinsky (1882–1971) was also an innovator and his *L'Histoire d'un soldat* (1918) was scored for clarinet, bassoon, cornet, trombone, violin, double bass, three actors and a dancer.

However, it will take a lot to beat Schoenberg's scoring of *Pierrot Lunaire*

ABOVE: Florilegium *was founded in 1991 to play the music of the 17th and 18th centuries. The group is one of the most exuberant chamber ensembles in Europe.*

ABOVE: An 18th-century string quartet playing at double music desks that are reminiscent of the double prayer desks of two centuries earlier.

specialized individuals, and might offer little to the amateur performer, who instead takes refuge in more accessible works from earlier eras.

String quartet

This chamber group was evolved by Joseph Haydn while he was employed by the Esterházy family at Eisenstadt near Vienna in the late 1750s. For the first time, chamber music abandoned the harpsichord and the new ensemble may have been used for outdoor serenades, for which it was too much trouble to carry the harpsichord outside. Altogether, Haydn wrote over 70 quartets, most of them in sets of six.

One of the novel features of the string quartet was that all the instruments had an equal share of the tunes, and for this reason the music was fun to play.

ABOVE: The San Francisco-based Kronos Quartet was founded in 1973 and exclusively devotes itself to playing music of the 20th century and beyond.

in 1912. This extraordinary work was written for flute, clarinet, bass clarinet, violin, viola, cello, piano and a narrator. The inflexions of the latter's voice are included in the score.

Modern chamber music

In the 20th century a reaction against the large Romantic orchestrations of the 19th century led to a renewed interest in chamber music. This was not the chamber music of the past, such as piano trios, string quartets and quintets, but small groups with new sounds and unusual combinations of instruments, with an emphasis on mixed ensembles of wind and strings and often also with vocal as well as percussion elements.

Modern chamber music has moved from the private house to the concert hall, and organizations such as the Library of Congress and the Dutch Donemus Foundation, or wealthy

individuals such as Walter Cobbett have been, and still are, active in promoting it.

The original social function and context of chamber music has now wholly disappeared. Much modern chamber music can be both difficult to play and demanding to listen to. It is often written for highly skilled and

ABOVE: Although piano duets using one or two pianos are common, it is most unusual for more than two to be played together. This photograph from a 1920s advertisement shows four musicians, each playing a Bechstein grand piano.

ABOVE: An early 19th-century quartet playing at a quadruple music desk especially designed for quartets.

This is still the case today: the sign of a good string quartet is a sense of equality.

The string quartet (like the brass band) suffers from a lack of colour contrasts – but this can be overcome not only by the differences in tone between the instruments, but by the way they are played. For instance, the instruments can be either played with the bow (*coll'arco*) or plucked with the fingers (*pizzicato*). The violin player may play notes on the G string that would normally be played on other strings. This gives a warmer quality to the sound.

Another trick to thicken the sound is the use of double-stopping, in which more than one string is played on an instrument at the same time. Two composers who used double-stopping to great effect were Debussy and Grieg. Contrasts can also be achieved by resting instruments before bringing them all in together for a climax. Haydn, Mozart and Beethoven were all masters of the string quartet and often doubled instruments for special effects.

In the 18th century it was taken for granted that music should be composed with amateur capabilities in mind. However, if a composer writes simple music today it is sometimes frowned upon and regarded as fit only for learner musicians. Although Mozart, Beethoven and Schubert all enjoyed writing string quartets, the form died out in the 19th century, but was revived in the 20th century, notably by Bartók and Shostakovich. Other 20th-century composers who are noted for their string quartets are Schoenberg, Hindemith, Walton and Tippett, whose five quartets included influences from the 16th-century madrigal.

Chamber orchestras

After World War I, economic factors saw an end to some of the large orchestras that had been dominant at the beginning of the 20th century, and composers increasingly wrote for smaller combinations of instruments. In the decades between the two World Wars a number of chamber orchestras were founded, the best known of which was the Basle Chamber Orchestra, which was set up in 1926 and was conducted by Paul Sacher.

In London, the Boyd Neel String Orchestra was founded in 1933. In an attempt to get the best of both worlds, it adopted an 18th-century repertoire and instrumentation while at the same time encouraging contemporary composers to write new works for it. In an attempt to stimulate interest in chamber music, similar orchestras, such as the Swiss Melos Ensemble, were founded all over Europe.

ABOVE: The English Chamber Orchestra was founded by Arnold Goldsbrough in 1948. One of its prime engagements was under Benjamin Britten at the Aldeburgh Festival.

ABOVE: The Austrian Alban Berg String Quartet was founded in 1971 and has won international distinction with its recordings of the complete Bach, Brahms, Berg and Webern quartets. They are seen here playing at the Royal Festival Hall, London, in 1998.

European National Music

Tell me where you live,
and I will tell you how you compose.

ROBERT SCHUMANN (1810–1856)

The 19th century was a period of European nationalism, not just in military matters but also in the arts, including music. For two centuries, the dominant musical figures in Europe had been German – from Bach to Beethoven – but the Romantic movement, which stressed personal feelings, led to composers striving to express their own traditions, and drawing on the musical influences of their own countries.

United Kingdom

Since the death of Henry Purcell in 1695, the United Kingdom had not produced a major composer, but the successful career of Arthur Sullivan (1842–1900), composer of the Savoy Operas, revived British music and paved the way for a generation of recognizably "English" voices, notably Edward Elgar (1857–1934) in whose music a mixture of nobility and nostalgia defined the British spirit at the end of the Victorian era. Frederick Delius (1862–1934) wrote works full of pastoral lyricism, and Ralph Vaughan Williams (1872–1958) rediscovered and reworked the rich vein of English folk music.

Czechoslovakia

One of the first orchestral composers to compose works with a definite national character was Bedřich Smetana (1824–84). Although he seldom used actual folk songs in his music, unlike his close friend Antonín Dvořák

(1841–1904), Smetana's work was unmistakably Czech. Absorbing the traditions of Berlioz and Liszt, Smetana was also an excellent pianist in the style of Clara Schumann. In 1861 he was appointed head of the Department of Music in the newly formed Prague

ABOVE: Scandinavian scenery inspired composers such as Sibelius and Grieg.

Society of Arts and it was during the tenure of this office that he wrote his most famous opera, *The Bartered Bride*. After suffering for some time from a whistling in his ears, in 1874 Smetana suddenly became stone deaf, but, like Beethoven before him, went on composing, including arguably his best work, *Má Vlast* ("My Country"), a set of six musical landscapes.

Finland

Another 19th-century composer whose music is evocative of his country is the Scandinavian Jean Sibelius (1865–1957), who was born in the

ABOVE: Sir Edward Elgar was England's greatest national composer of the 20th century. His work includes such typically English compositions as the four Pomp and Circumstance *marches and the* Enigma Variations. *A great friend of Adrian Boult, Elgar fixed a sign on his cottage gate, "Please Boult the Gate".*

Finnish town of Hämeenlinna. Although intended for a legal career, he soon abandoned his law studies to devote himself entirely to music. In 1892 a performance of his first large-scale orchestral work, the *Kullervo* Symphony, created such a sensation that he soon became established as Finland's leading composer. One of his most popular works is the tone poem *Finlandia*, which he composed in 1899 and which was banned by the Tsar because it roused such nationalistic fervour. Although his inspiration was intimately connected with Finnish landscape and literature (such as *Kalevala*, the national folk epic), Sibelius's achievements lie principally in his remarkable mastery of form.

Norway
Edvard Grieg (1843–1907) turned to his native folk music for inspiration, having learnt the folk songs of Norway from his mother. One of his most popular works is his incidental music to Ibsen's play *Peer Gynt*, in which he evokes trolls, mists and mountains in a work that is unmistakably Scandinavian.

Germany
One of the most obvious examples of overt nationalism in 19th-century orchestral music must be the work of Richard Wagner (1813–83), whose love of everything Aryan was to make him the darling of the Nazis, who conveniently forgot his Semitic ancestry. Wagner drew inspiration from

ABOVE: In the 18th and 19th centuries Prague was one of the main musical capitals of Europe. This scene of the Old Square is as it was in the days when Mozart walked its streets, and would have been familiar to Czechoslovakia's two great national composers, Dvořák and Smetana.

ABOVE: The Battle of Polotsk, 18 August, 1812. One of the compositions that most brings to mind "Mother Russia" is Tchaikovsky's 1812 Overture, which describes in music the day when Napoleon's army was finally defeated. The work has many musical effects, from the roar of cannon to church bells ringing out the news of victory.

the legends and myths of Germanic folklore, producing epic operas such as *Tristan und Isolde* and *Tannhäuser,* as well as the renowned *Der Ring des Nibelungen*.

France
Camille Saint-Saëns (1835–1921), as president of the Société Nationale de Musique, declared himself in favour of the "essential French qualities of logic, reason and clarity", and imparted these qualities to his huge musical output, including operas, choral and orchestral works, organ and chamber music. Gabriel Fauré (1845–1924) was a pupil of Saint-Saëns, and composed ravishing songs and choral works of great delicacy and elegance.

Russia
Russian music is full of the sounds of "Mother Russia", from Tchaikovsky's patriotic *1812 Overture* to the folk-based compositions of musicians such as Mikhail Glinka (1804–57). Glinka was regarded as the "father" of Russian music, and inspired a group of composers, known as "The Five", who set out to develop a pure Russian style. They included Alexander Borodin (1833–87), whose opera *Prince Igor* relates the story of the 12th-century struggles of the Russians against the Polovtsy invaders, and Modest Mussorgsky (1839–81) whose masterpiece is the opera *Boris Godunov*, based on Pushkin's drama about the 16th-century Tsar.

Folk Music

The best way to get to knowing any bunch of people
is to go and listen to their music.

WOODY GUTHRIE (1912–67)

While most music tends to cross boundaries, folk music differs from area to area. The folk music of Northumberland is different from that of southern England; the music of Hamburg is different from that of Munich or the Tyrol; in Russia, the folk tunes in the west are different from those in the east. The workers on the American cotton plantations sang songs that were unknown in the industrial cities of Boston and New York. The words and tunes of folk songs were transmitted aurally, and might have existed in several versions in different places, as they were subtly altered over the years.

In Britain, most songs were traditionally sung only by men. Women exercised their vocal chords only while working or in the home, and were very rarely heard in public.

ABOVE: This print from the 1830s shows a party of villagers folk-dancing outside an inn in Süd Tirol, Austria, now part of northern Italy.

Work songs

Many traditional songs were about work, especially the hard conditions associated with occupations such as working in the fields, down the mines or on ships. Singing made hard work easier and many songs were of the call and response type, in which the leader or shantyman would sing out the story and the rest of the workers would join in the chorus. Another type of work song was the street cry, with which street vendors advertised their wares.

Ballads

The ballad was a song that told a story, and might be based on contemporary news events of the day, such as a battle or a mining disaster, or on legends or fictional tales. In the days before radio or television, when few working people were able to read newspapers, singing or listening to these ballads was one way to escape briefly from the

ABOVE: The composer Béla Bartók travelled extensively all over Hungary and neighbouring states, making recordings of folk songs.

daily grind. There were also many shorter songs, which might be pithy and humorous or lyrical and romantic.

Instrumental accompaniment

At work in the fields, or in the home, most folk music was sung unaccompanied. In Biblical Israel songs were sung to the accompaniment of the harp, while in classical Greece the singer was accompanied on the kithara. In medieval Europe folk songs were sung to pipe and tabor and later to the hurdy-gurdy or bagpipes. Bagpipes were purely a folk instrument, being thought to be crude and fit only for the tavern, in contrast to the viol, favoured by the more well-to-do.

Dancing

Feast days and their associated rituals have invariably included both music and dancing, such as the May Day Morris dancing of southern England and the sword dances of the north. These two very different traditions of folk-dancing reflect the Viking occupation of the north-east of Britain.

Originally, dances like these were performed only on certain occasions, and were part of religious ceremonies to celebrate the passing of the seasons and to bring good luck to the harvest. Though the original significance of these dances has been lost, they are

ABOVE: Before radio and television people made their own amusements, and one of the few pastimes available for the "labouring poor" was dancing. This print of 1804 shows a Polish man dancing before his friends.

ABOVE: One of the joys of life in the southern states of America is when the family play their instruments on the porch.

ABOVE: Morris dancing is thought to be associated with fertility. There are many groups who try to recreate England's past.

still performed on festive occasions, such as village fête days.

Some folk dances have become popularized far beyond their point of origin. The waltz originated as a peasant dance in southern Germany, but has become known – in its more refined state – all over the world. Another genre that has become popular way beyond its native shores, due both to migration and, latterly, to a film and stage show, is Irish dancing.

As with folk songs, the instruments that provided the music for these dances were small and portable, such as the fiddle. The accordion, invented in the early 19th century, became popular as an accompaniment for open-air dancing, and a 20th-century innovation in Morris sides is the inclusion of the concertina.

Contemporary folk music

In the 1960s, with the growth of the American civil rights movement and the increasing aversion of young people to America's involvement in the war in Vietnam, folk songs experienced a

revival of interest as a means of political protest, sung by professional folk singers such as Joan Baez (born 1941), Pete Seeger (born 1919) and Bob Dylan (born 1941). Many of Bob Dylan's "protest" songs of the mid '60s have become folk classics, such as *Masters of War*, *The Times They are A-changin'* and *With God on our Side*. Country Joe McDonald's chorus, "And it's one, two, three, what are we fighting for?" has become the universal anti-war anthem.

ABOVE: One of the new-style folk singers of the 1960s was Bob Dylan, whose songs relate to the protest movement of that time.

Revolutionary Music of the 20th Century

Think nothing. Wait until it is absolutely still within you.
When you have attained this begin to play.

KARLHEINZ STOCKHAUSEN, INSTRUCTIONS TO PERFORMERS OF "ES"

As the 20th century dawned, some composers turned away from the hitherto accepted rules of harmony and composition and ventured out into the realms of polytonality, atonality and microtones.

Atonal music

In 1908 the Austrian composer Arnold Schoenberg (1874–1951) changed the whole basis of harmony. He abandoned

By numbers

A composer who drew inspiration from unusual sources was the Russian Joseph Schillinger, who emigrated to the United States in 1930. At one concert he asked his audience which composer the new work he had just played reminded them of. Suggestions included Mozart, Bach and Beethoven; however, nobody could guess Schillinger's actual source, which had been the stock-market quotations. Schillinger had plotted the figures on a sheet of graph paper and given each a proportional musical value. Schillinger also taught music, and amongst his pupils was Glenn Miller, whose *Moonlight Serenade* was written as an exercise set by Schillinger.

ABOVE: *Arnold Schoenberg decided to abandon tonality in 1907 when he wrote his Second String Quartet, a work in which the keys are not stated but "sensed".*

the idea of the central keynote and regarded every semitone of a chromatic scale as being of equal importance. One of his early atonal compositions was the opera *Expectation*, a work for soprano and orchestra. Although some listeners admired Schoenberg's work, many more found it unintelligible, preferring tonal music that was more pleasing to the ear.

Microtones

Another innovation of the 20th century was the use of microtones. Although microtones were, and still are, common in eastern music, and are found in some eastern European folk music, the smallest interval generally

used in European music was the semitone. The main promoter of microtones in Europe was the Czech composer Alois Hába (born 1893), who divided the notes of the scale into intervals of one-third, one-quarter and one-sixth of a tone. Due to the construction of European wind instruments, such music is only easily playable on strings and trombones.

Polytonal music

Polytonality is the use of two keys simultaneously. Again, to most listeners this is very grating on the ear, but the genre did find some early supporters. One of these was Charles Ives (1874–1954), an insurance salesman who wrote music in his spare time. Some of his music is very complex to perform: in its original form, his Fourth Symphony, for instance, needs four conductors to

ABOVE: *Charles Ives was the first American composer to break away from the German style that had influenced most American music during the late 19th century.*

ABOVE: *Dimitri Shostakovich was greatly influenced by his compatriots Rimsky-Korsakov, Tchaikovsky and Prokofiev.*

keep the players together. Another exponent of polytonality was Igor Stravinsky. His music for the ballet *The Rite of Spring* begins with a bassoon solo that is scored deliberately at the top of the instrument's range because he wanted the player to strive to reach the note to give the sound the quality of struggle. At its first performance in Paris in May 1913 the audience almost caused a riot. At one point the manager of the theatre, in an attempt to restore calm, was heard to say "Listen before you boo." When the composer Camille Saint-Saëns heard the work, he just kept repeating *"Il est fou."* Yet the work has since become an established and popular part of the orchestral repertoire.

Aleatoric music

Some of the music of Karlheinz Stockhausen (born 1928) never sounds the same twice over because it is aleatoric: it includes the improvisatory elements of chance and free choice. Stockhausen has abandoned conventional notation altogether and writes "text scores" in which he explains in words how the music should be played. In *Gold Dust*, for instance, he even suggests that the musicians should starve themselves for four days and nights before the performance.

Another composer who explored the operation of chance was John Cage (1912–92), whose *4' 33"* consists of

four minutes and 33 seconds of silence, the idea being that the music is created by the sounds provided by the natural environment at the time. This work was satirized by the musician and humorist Gerard Hoffnung, who in the mid 1950s announced that he had written a work that included three bars of silence. The first and third bars, so Hoffnung explained, were in 5:4 time, but the second bar was in 3:4 time, "thereby giving the whole work a quasi-Viennese flavour".

ABOVE: *Karlheinz Stockhausen abandoned both conventional musical notation and instrumentation, utilizing "instruments" such as iron chains and shortwave radios.*

ABOVE: *Igor Stravinsky had a rich and diverse musical output. Here he is shown conducting a 1951 rehearsal of his opera* The Rake's Progress *in Venice, Italy.*

Many of Cage's works for dance companies and concert performances exploited his invention of the "prepared piano", in which he created percussive effects by placing objects such as rubber bands and paperclips between the strings. He also wrote *HPSCHD*, a piece for seven harpsichords and 51 tape machines, and *0'00"* which was for any musician playing any instrument in any way.

ABOVE: *The composer and pianist John Cage was a pupil of Schoenberg. His music exploits a variety of percussive and novel sound effects produced by orthodox instruments, modified instruments such as the "prepared" piano, and objects such as radio receivers, chairs and even dead fish.*

Brass Bands

The brass band contest is the one and only
successful rival to the football match.

GEORGE MILLER

Brass bands came into existence in England and Wales in the 1830s as a result of the philanthropic efforts of factory owners to enrich the lives of their work forces. They saw brass bands as valuable adjuncts to their works, and in an era of increasing leisure, the bands became a popular pastime.

Improvement in the manufacture of brass instruments at around this time made both fingering and blowing easier, and the advent of the railways made travel feasible for working people. It was not long before bands began to compete with one another in friendly rivalry.

ABOVE: *Brass baritones from an Austrian town band giving an outdoor performance in Salzburg, Austria.*

Contests

The first known brass band contest, at which five bands took part, was held at Burton Constable, near Hull, in 1845. In those early days the participating bands were restricted to 12 players (as opposed to 25 today) and played arrangements of works by composers such as Weber, Rossini and Mozart.

The most distinguished of these early bandsmen was Enderby Jackson, a conductor and arranger who, in 1854, established the principle that all participating bands in a contest should play the same test piece.

Today the British National Brass Band Contest, held in London at the Royal Albert Hall, is the highlight of the British bandsman's year. Since 1978 the more ambitious British bands have also been able to compete with their European counterparts at the European Brass Band Championships.

United States and beyond

Brass bands became popular in the United States almost as early as they did in Britain. One of the first bands to be formed in the United States was the Brass Band of New York, established by Alan Dodworth in 1834. Brass band

ABOVE: *The "Besses o' th' Barn" band from Whitefield, Lancashire, was one of England's foremost brass bands. It was founded in 1818 and is seen here during its successful tour of France in 1905.*

concerts soon became a part of the American way of life. It was truly music for the people, with bandstand gazebos in almost every park. Some of these, such as that in New York's Central Park, were paid for by the railway company as a way of increasing fare income by transporting out-of-town concertgoers into the city. On Boston Common, concerts were so well attended that some are said to have attracted crowds of up to 10,000 people.

By 1900 the brass band movement had reached its zenith in England and Wales, with some 20,000 brass bands. Although their number declined after World War II, there was a revival of interest from the 1960s. This resurgence occurred not only in Britain, Australia, New Zealand and the United States but also in Europe, where British-style brass bands were formed in the Netherlands, Sweden, Switzerland, Norway and Belgium.

Repertoire

Brass bands play a mixture of transcriptions of orchestral works and original compositions. Notable early

ABOVE: The Durham Miners' Gala is one of the most eagerly anticipated events in the British brass bandsman's diary. Many bands take part in the event, both marching through the town and giving static concerts.

arrangers of music for bands include J. Ord Hume, Samuel Cope and William Rimmer. As well as orchestral composers such as Arthur Bliss, Gustav Holst and Sir Edward Elgar, all of whom wrote for brass band, the brass band's repertoire has been greatly enhanced by men such as Eric

Ball, Geoffrey Brand and Granville Bantock. At first, some of this new music was treated with suspicion, and it was not unknown for band conductors, unaccustomed to anything but the harmonies of marches and hymn tunes, to change "wrong notes" to their own satisfaction. It is reported that one conductor with a limited knowledge of Italian went into a music shop after receiving a new score with the intention of buying "some of those new-fangled *senza mutes*".

These days, band concerts in the park are still enjoyed by thousands of people who like nothing better than relaxing in the sunshine listening to a "good drop of music".

LEFT: The continued survival of brass bands in Britain depends on young people taking up brass instruments to fill the ranks of older musicians. The presence of so many youth bands in the country assures the future of the brass band movement.

Military Bands

Explain it as we may, a martial strain
will urge a man into the front rank of battle.

HENRY THEODORE TUCKERMAN (1813–71)

Soldiers of the world have always marched to music, even if it was only the rhythmic tread of their own feet. By 1600 BC Egyptians were marching to trumpet and drum, and a thousand years later Roman trumpeters played on the march. Trumpets were an integral part of Caesar's army and on that fateful day, while standing by the bridge crossing the Rubicon, the trumpets blew a thunderous blast. In 6th-century Persia the regiments marched to bands of drums, pipes and trumpets. Four hundred years later their descendants were still enjoying the stirring music of large bands of drums, cymbals, trumpets and other wind instruments.

European military bands

Military bands came to the attention of western Europeans during the Crusades from the 11th to 13th centuries, when they encountered Saracen bands consisting of *surnay* (oboes), *nafir* (trumpets), *buq* (horns) and *naqqara* (kettledrums). During the late Middle Ages European armies began to copy these bands loosely, employing combinations of shawms, bagpipes, trumpets and drums. The duties of the musicians were mainly to play at tournaments and to accompany the soldiers on campaign.

Janissary bands

An important development during the 18th century was the adoption by European military bands of "Turkish" or "Janissary" music. The instrumentation of these bands included oboes, fifes, side drums, kettledrums, cymbals, triangles, Turkish crescent and bass drum. Such was the fad for this type of music that some regiments in Poland, Russia and Prussia even imported whole bands, complete with musicians, from Turkey. Today, remnants of the Janissary era live on in the leopardskin apron worn by bass drummers and the shape of the lyre glockenspiel.

The trend was reversed in the early 19th century when, in 1826, the Sultan of Turkey disbanded his corps of Janissaries and invited Giuseppe Donizetti (brother of the composer) to reorganize Turkish bands on the lines

ABOVE: *Russian horn bands were a feature of the late 18th and early 19th centuries. Such*
was the popularity of these combinations with the Russian nobility that they often sold them
to one another — players as well as horns.

ABOVE: *For centuries, armies have used drums to keep their marching troops in step. Here an 18th-century side drummer leads a platoon of troops past the National Theatre in Prague.*

ABOVE: *Brightly dressed army side drummers playing at the Battle of Fontenoy in 1745.*

of European ones. Persian bands followed suit and adopted Western instrumentation in about 1840.

New instruments

By the end of the 18th century military bands were increasing in size, mainly as a result of adding extra percussion instruments, which in turn made it necessary – for purposes of audibility – to increase the wind section. Clarinets, both B flat and E flat, were introduced into military bands and soon

outnumbered any other instrument. Performing the same role as the violins in the symphony orchestra, there were two main reasons for the clarinet replacing the oboe in military bands. First, it is much easier for a marching musician to play the single reed clarinet than the double reed oboe and

second, the softer sound of the oboe tends to become lost when playing with modern brass instruments.

American Civil War bands

During the American Civil War military bands proliferated on both sides of the conflict and were heard on all occasions, from ceremonial parades to battle marches. A good band was a source of tremendous pride and was long remembered by those fortunate enough to witness the "dawn of peace".

Sometimes Union bands played in competition with their southern counterparts. One such impromptu concert happened during a lull in the Battle of Spotsylvania in 1864. Each side brought their band to the front line where, for an hour or so, the bands played alternate tunes. The concert ended with the Confederate band bringing tears to the eyes of the battle-hardened men of both sides with their heart-rending rendition of *Home Sweet Home*.

ABOVE: *Members of military bands often "double" on stringed instruments. The bands of the Austrian Empire were no exception and here Johann Strauss the Younger is seen conducting a military orchestra at a royal ball in Vienna.*

Military schools of music

A major event in the evolution of European military bands was the celebration of peace at the end of the Crimean War in 1856. Military bands of all the allied nations took part, giving the bandsmen an opportunity to hear each other play and compare standards. In the wake of the British bands' poor showing (particularly embarrassing when they played the national anthem in different keys), the Royal Military School of Music was founded at Kneller Hall in Twickenham, near London.

At this time British military bandmasters were still mainly civilian musicians and – more surprisingly – were in many cases foreign. Three examples were Francis Ptacek, a member of the Prague Conservatoire who was director of the band of the Leicestershire Militia; Herr Sawerthal,

ABOVE: Marching bands are popular in the United States, Australia and, to a lesser degree, Britain. This Sydney annual marching band festival takes place in Australia every August.

the bandmaster of the Royal Engineers; and Karl Tieke, the composer of the evergreen march *Alte Kameraden*, who was the director of the band of the Royal Irish Dragoon Guards.

It was not until 1887 that an army bandmaster, Dan Godfrey, the director of the band of the Grenadier Guards, received a commission. Today all directors of full-time military bands are of officer rank.

Civilian "military" bands

During the 19th century the term "military band" became something of a misnomer as it began to be used more loosely, referring also to civilian bands using military band instrumentation for public concerts. One of the most popular of these civilian bands was the renowned Jullien Band.

Jullien

Louis Antoine Jullien (1812–60) was the son of a military bandsman. After a period of study at the Paris Conservatoire, he began promoting concerts of dance music at the Jardin Ture, where he became known as the "Napoleon of Music".

ABOVE: Almost every school in the United States has its own band. This one is proudly playing on the steps of the Capitol building in Washington DC.

ABOVE: The drum corps of the Grenadier Guards playing at the annual "Trooping of the Colour" in London.

ABOVE: One of the best-known annual events in Germany is the Oktoberfest. *Held in Munich, this beer festival is enlivened by the many bands that perform.*

father's footsteps and became a professional trombonist, but later turned to the violin and conducting. Between 1868 and 1892 he built up a promising reputation as bandmaster of the United States Marine Corps Band. In 1892 he left the service to form his own famous band, which toured Europe several times as well as making a two-year world tour in 1910–11. Sousa, who is justly called the "March King", composed 136 marches, including *The Washington Post*, *The Stars and Stripes Forever*, *Liberty Bell*, *High School Cadets* and *El Capitan*. Sousa is also remembered for the redesigned helicon first made for his band in 1899, now known as the sousaphone.

In 1840 he moved to England, and made his debut in Drury Lane in June.

Thanks to a spotless white waistcoat, as well as his ambrosial curls, superb moustache and the magnificent air with which he wielded his baton, Jullien was the object of unsparing ridicule.

He was a devotee of Beethoven, and whenever he conducted works by that composer he would have a new pair of white gloves presented to him which he would wear while he conducted.

Each year Jullien tried to bring some novelty into his concerts. In 1849 he introduced the *monstre* ophicleide (a brass instrument later superseded by the tuba) which at that time was the largest wind instrument ever made. In 1851 he toured with a French drum corps, which appeared in full military uniform by permission of Prince Louis Napoleon. In the same year, appreciating the discomforts, if not the dangers, of passive smoking, Jullien requested that his concerts be non-smoking events.

Sousa

Another famous civilian wind band was that formed by John Philip Sousa (1854–1932) in 1892. Sousa was born in Washington DC, and from the age of six he learnt to play the violin, as well as studying various band instruments, harmony and musical theory. In 1867 he followed in his

ABOVE: Jullien's concerts were always sold out well in advance. Despite this, he was never able to pay off the debts he had amassed in Paris, and he died bankrupt.

ABOVE: Sousa was justly known as the "March King" — he composed 136 marches. His band became famous worldwide and he made a two-year world tour in 1910–11.

Country Music

*You got to have smelt a lot of mule manure
before you can sing like a hillbilly.*

HANK WILLIAMS (1923–53)

For many, country music is summed up as songs about orphaned children, lost mothers, betrayed lovers, train wrecks and coal-mining disasters. However, there is actually a lot more to country music than sentimentality and sickly patriotism. It is not just "hillbilly music" but has a century of tradition, with many styles evolving and co-existing over the decades. It is a blending of the two distinct traditions of the American settlers: European ballads, story songs and dance music, and African-American blues and work songs.

ABOVE: Hank Williams was America's greatest honky-tonk performer, whose early death ensured him a permanent place in country music's pantheon of stars. One of his best-known songs is Cold, Cold Heart.

The commercialization of this blend came in the mid 19th century with the minstrel shows that were created by white performers parodying black manners. These shows gave birth to two distinct forms of entertainment. In the North they evolved into vaudeville, while in the South they nurtured home-grown banjo and fiddle players.

Another seedbed for country music was the southern rural church where singing was – and still is – a central part of the service. Although the white and black churches had different styles, they merged into a tightly harmonized music called "bluegrass". An early example of this type of music was that sung by the Carter Family from Virginia, whose songs were based on the ultimate embodiment of home and family values. Their unornamented, nasal, simple four-square harmonies were entirely white with no black influences whatsoever.

In marked contrast to the "home harmonizers", there were more progressive singers, such as Jimmie Rodgers (1897–1933), who sang a combination of jazz, blues and country. Although he recorded with many bands, his most moving performances were those in which he was accompanied only by his guitar – songs such as the autobiographical *T. B. Blues*, *T. for Texas* and *Waitin' for a Train*, which is one of the most popular train songs ever.

ABOVE: The fiddle is one of the most popular instruments with country musicians. It is used in many types of country music, from bluegrass to the sentimental tones accompanying the songs for which the genre is famous.

ABOVE: This country fiddle player is being accompanied by an accordion player.

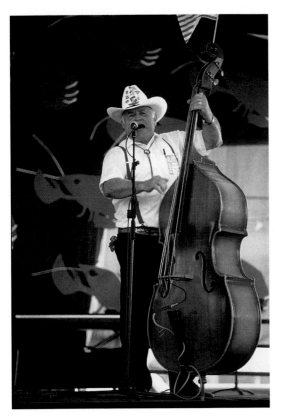

ABOVE: Before the advent of the electric bass guitar, every country band had a string bass. Some bass players were very versatile and were able to produce remarkable effects on their instrument.

pianos and a strong string section, became known throughout the world. Nashville remained the bastion of country music throughout the 1960s, but remained very conservative, both artistically and politically. In the '60s and early '70s there was, for example, an unhealthy number of songs supporting America's involvement in the Vietnam War, notably Merle Haggard's *Okie from Muskogee* and *The Fightin' Side of Me*, which cemented his stardom but enraged liberals everywhere. The slushy sounds of Nashville were rejected by singers such as Waylon Jennings (who had played with Buddy Holly) and Willie Nelson. They left Nashville and went to Texas where they established what has become known as "outlaw country". During the 1980s and '90s mainstream country music has become more and more like pop, so that in many cases it is hard to spot the difference.

ABOVE: Willie Nelson (born 1933) is one of the most influencial songwriters and singers country music has ever known. His laid-back style of singing once led one reviewer to announce that by the time Nelson had sung one line, Dolly Parton would have sung a complete song! One of Nelson's best-known albums is Tougher than Leather, *which deals with the effects of fate on life.*

Rodgers influenced many country singers, including the legendary Hank Williams (1923–53). Williams sang in the first person and dealt head-on with issues such as adultery and alcoholism. His many songs are still part of almost every country singer's repertoire and there is hardly ever a country music concert anywhere that does not include at least one Hank Williams song.

Grand Ole Opry
Country music spread into the homes of Americans via radio programmes, in particular Chicago's *National Barn Dance*, the *Louisiana Hayride* from Shreveport, and WSM Radio's *Grand Ole Opry* from Nashville, Tennessee. In the mid 1950s Nashville became the centre of country music and the "Nashville Sound", featuring tickling

ABOVE: Many solo country singers have teamed up with a colleague to produce duets. One of the most successful of such pairings is Dolly Parton and Kenny Rogers.

Jazz

If you're in jazz and more than ten people like you,
you're labelled commercial.

HERBIE MANN (BORN 1930)

Jazz is a truly American music, being a combination of that country's two dominant cultures – African and European. As a genre it is almost unique in embodying both rural and urban sounds, as well as ranging from the raw sounds of New Orleans Dixieland bands to the sophistication of New York cool jazz groups.

New Orleans

Dixieland jazz evolved from the ragtime music of the late 19th century, which was epitomized by the work of Scott Joplin, composer of piano rags such as *The Entertainer*. Finding the steady ragtime 2:4 time monotonous, some musicians doubled the time to 4:4 and began to play the melody just a little ahead of or behind the beat, which gave an unevenness to the pulse.

ABOVE: Louis Armstrong single-handedly transformed jazz from a collective art to one of solo expression. His clear, ringing trumpet-playing was impeccable.

These subtle rhythmic changes increased the swing of the music, producing the fast, happy, high-energy music now known as traditional jazz.

One of the earliest exponents of the genre was Buddy Bolden (1877–1931), who is remembered for his blues songs, such as *Careless Love*. Another of the early traditional players was Jelly Roll Morton (1885–1941), a brilliant pianist, arranger and composer, who is best remembered for his *Tiger Rag*.

Another early New Orleans bandleader was "King" Oliver (1885–1938), who moved to Chicago in 1918 and formed his own band, the Creole Jazz Band, in 1922. One of the musicians Oliver invited to join him was Louis Armstrong (1901–71), who had started his professional life playing trumpet in the red-light district of New Orleans for 15 cents a night. Armstrong, a master of improvisation, formed his own band in 1925 and revolutionized jazz for all time. He was the first to create solo improvised melodies that complemented the basic theme, and thus established the central role of the soloist in what had previously been an ensemble form. His technical virtuosity was breathtaking – he was, for instance, able to hold high notes effortlessly for three or four bars at a time.

Chicago "traditional" jazz

Influenced by what was happening in New Orleans, the Chicago of the early 1900s was also a centre of jazz. Led by Nick LaRocca, the Original Dixieland Jazz Band — which was composed

ABOVE: When one thinks of jazz, one automatically thinks of New Orleans, a city where almost every bar and club has its own house band.

melodic improvisation is very free in cool jazz and players often use counterpoint to play two improvised melodic lines at the same time. Two of the best-known exponents of cool jazz are Miles Davis (1926–91) and the Dave Brubeck Quartet.

ABOVE: *As well as being a comedian and film maker, Woody Allen is an enthusiastic jazz clarinettist, his favourite being New Orleans jazz. He is seen here guesting in a band show.*

ABOVE: *Thelonious Monk was one of the greatest jazz pianists. Born in New York City, he began playing at his local Baptist church. Although he had his own big band, he is better known for his jazz quartet.*

solely of white musicians – made the first ever jazz recordings in 1917. One man who was inspired by the band was the legendary Bix Beiderbecke (1903–31) who, after hearing a recording by LaRocca, persuaded his parents to give him a cornet. He formed his own band – the Wolverines – in 1923, but by 1925 he had gone solo and was performing with various touring bands. Although he died at only 28, Beiderbecke was the man chiefly responsible for introducing Dixieland jazz to a white audience, and without him the genre would never have become so popular.

Bebop and cool jazz

An offshoot of classical jazz is bebop, which developed in Harlem in the early 1940s. The onomatopoeic name was coined by young musicians including Dizzy Gillespie (1917–93), Charlie Parker (1920–55) and Thelonious Monk (1917–82) to describe the style that emerged during their jam sessions, characterized by upbeat rhythms, fast tempo and improvisation. Bebop later became accepted as the nickname for the

whole wave of new jazz that exploded after World War II.

Cool jazz ("modern jazz") musicians take a more intellectual approach to their music. Disdaining any kind of showmanship, they often play with their backs to the audience. The rhythm is muted, the drummer simply keeping the beat, on which the players stay rather than syncopating. The

ABOVE: *Dizzy Gillespie, trumpeter, composer and bandleader, was responsible for giving jazz a whole new style that included whole-tone scales and altered chords.*

Big Bands

To swing is to affirm.

Father G. V. Kennard

In the mid 1920s the move began to form larger jazz bands, which were in fact small orchestras. Two of the early dance bands of the era were those led by Paul Whiteman (1890–1967) and Fletcher Henderson (1897–1952).

Whiteman, a classically trained violinist, formed his first (all-white) small band in 1919. In 1924 he organized the first ever concert of jazz music at New York's Aeolian Hall, at which the highlight was George Gershwin playing his *Rhapsody in Blue* for the first time. Whiteman's orchestra was so successful that at one time there were no less than 28 different "Whiteman" bands touring the United States.

Fletcher Henderson, whose band consisted of all black musicians,

ABOVE: *Glenn Miller formed his band in 1938, and within a year his trademark sound of soothing reeds – for example in* In The Mood *– had become world famous.*

played at New York's Roseland Ballroom. However in 1923, after Louis Armstrong had played for a short time with the band, Henderson changed his style from polite dance music to swing jazz. Henderson is remembered especially for his revolutionary "call and response" arrangements, which split the band's instruments into two groups, the first group stating a melody and the second responding to it.

Instrumentation

One of the important innovations of the big band was the introduction of the saxophone. One of the first jazz saxophonists was Coleman Hawkins (1904–69), who introduced the instrument to Henderson's band in

1923. Between the 1930s and '60s, saxophones were to feature strongly in the "big band" orchestras led by people such as Glenn Miller and Duke Ellington in the United States, Henry Hall in England and Bert Kaempfert and James Last in Germany.

Big band leaders

One of the most talented jazz musicians was Duke Ellington (1899–1974). His compositions are still standard works in most bands' repertoires and include classics such as *Satin Doll* and *Mood Indigo*. Ellington, whose band was at its peak during the 1930s, introduced the "jungle style", in which growling trumpets and wailing clarinets gave the music an unmistakable African feeling.

ABOVE: *George Gershwin was one of America's most versatile songwriters. With his brother Ira he wrote musical comedies, such as* Funny Face *and* Tiptoes.

ABOVE: *Duke Ellington: pianist, bandleader and composer.*

ABOVE: *Noted especially for his minimalist piano style, which he had perfected by the end of the 1930s, Count Basie was one of the finest jazz pianists of the 20th century.*

Another jazz man to hit the scene in the 1930s was the clarinettist Benny Goodman (1909–86). Goodman was well known for his sight-reading skills and was the first white jazz musician to break the colour barrier and work with black colleagues. Goodman's band, which was noted for being the best rehearsed and most precise, played the "pop" music of its day.

Kansas City swing

Count (William) Basie (1904–84), who became the leader of Kansas City swing, began his career as pianist in the Bennie Moten band, one of the first to feature the combination of five brass, four reed and four rhythm players. After Moten's death in 1935, Basie began to build his own ensemble from the remnants of his mentor's band. He soon became one of the most successful jazz bandleaders, and led his band until his death in 1984. The band was noted for its "head arranging", in which riffs were improvised during performances, the other musicians having hastily to adjust their parts.

Western swing

Western swing is a combination of string-band music with jazz styles that developed in the late 1920s. One of the first bands to feature the new type of music was the Light Crust Doughboys, which featured the fiddler Bob Wills (1905–75). Wills soon left to form his own band, the Texas Playboys, which became the epitome of western swing. Wills incorporated old-time country fiddling, jazz, blues, boogie-woogie and the Tex-Mex sounds that became so popular in the 1960s.

ABOVE: *Although the early days of Basie's band were exhilaratingly wild, under his leadership they became the most disciplined and sleek big band of the era.*

ABOVE: *Benny Goodman, the "King of Swing", was at home in jazz and classical music.*

ABOVE: *Duke Ellington was the master of swing and endured long after the period was history. He led arguably one of the greatest swing bands of all time.*

Rock and Pop

You have to blame Thomas Edison for today's rock 'n' roll.
He invented [sic] electricity.

STAN GETZ (1927–91)

Rock music evolved from the blues. After the end of World War II many African-Americans from the Deep South moved to northern cities such as Chicago, in search of work and to escape the racialism that was — and to some extent still is – rife in the former Confederate States. Here, musicians created an urbanized rhythm that served as a foundation for pioneer rock 'n' rollers such as Little Richard and Chuck Berry.

Electric guitar

Although the first solid-body electric guitar was built by Les Paul, it was first mass-produced by Leo Fender, and became a key element in rock 'n' roll. Fender, a California-based guitar and

ABOVE: Elvis Presley was the foremost and most influential popular singer of the 1950s and '60s. His style ranged from country to rock and mainstream.

ABOVE: The Beatles, who began their musical career in a nightclub in Liverpool, became the world's top pop group with hit records such as She Loves You *and* A Hard Day's Night.

amplifier manufacturer, had often been asked by musicians if he could give more volume and at the same time eliminate screech and feedback from the electrified instruments of the time. He came up with the solid-body guitar that he developed just after World War II. His first model, the Broadcaster, entered mass production in 1948, and its sharpness and attack made it an instant success, especially with country musicians. In 1950 its name was changed to the Telecaster, and it was this instrument that gave the rock of that decade its distinctive sound. In 1951 Fender introduced his solid-body bass guitar and, five years later, his futuristic Stratocaster.

One of the pioneers of electric guitar-playing was Muddy Waters (1915–83), who moved up to Chicago from Mississippi. In 1944 he bought his first electric guitar, one made by Fender, and within two years had formed his first electric combo.

African-American music

The importance of African-American music cannot be overestimated. From the Motown sound of the 1960s, through soul and disco to the rap of the 1990s, the exciting sounds of black music have dominated and led the way in many popular music trends. More than anything else, rock music has helped to integrate black and white America, breaking down the racial barrier that has plagued the country.

The 1950s

Many of the young white singers of the 1950s derived their inspiration from black music, including Elvis Presley (1935–77), who became one of the most influential rock 'n' roll singers of the 20th century. Born in Tupelo, Mississippi, as a boy Elvis was always in demand for singing at church services and revival meetings, and was greatly influenced by black blues singers. Indeed, when people who did not know him heard him singing, they could not believe that he was white. Presley's romantic, suggestive ballads, which were matched by his gyrations on stage, made him one of the first mass idols of American adolescent culture (as well as getting him banned from many television stations).

ABOVE: *The legendary rock guitarist Jimi Hendrix, born in Seattle, had his first hit in Britain with* Hey Joe *in 1967.*

Another pioneer was Buddy Holly (1936–59), whose short career was the inspiration for many singers of the 1960s, including Mick Jagger. Holly was a shy, bespectacled youth from Texas whose life was tragically cut short in a plane crash in 1959.

Rock 'n' roll was synonymous with rebellion and no one was more rebellious than Jerry Lee Lewis (born 1935), who shocked the morality of the age by marrying his 13-year-old cousin. It was not until the mid 1960s that Lewis once again gained public approval.

ABOVE: *Abba, whose name was taken from the initial letters of the members' names, were one of the few pop groups outside America or Britain to gain international stardom.*

Pop music

The 1960s have been rightly dubbed the "Swinging Sixties", and musically they were dominated by the Beatles and the Rolling Stones. Whereas the Beatles based their music on the rock of the 1950s, the Rolling Stones were rhythm-and-blues-based. Both bands had great success, and in one way or another have influenced almost every other rock band since.

While many bands were conventional, some performers mirrored the violence of the time (especially the United States' involvement in Vietnam). One of these was Jimi Hendrix (1942–70), who was one of the greatest guitarists of the '60s and had been a member of James Brown's backing band, the Famous Flames. His erotic stage actions, suggestive lyrics and guitar-smashing antics brought him much criticism – on one occasion he doused his guitar with lighter fuel and set it on fire. Other like-minded bands included The Who and the Sex Pistols.

ABOVE: *Frank Zappa (1940–1993) started writing music at high school, inspired by the rhythmic experimentation of the avant-garde composer Edgar Varèse.*

ABOVE: *Vanessa Mae (born 1976) became one of the youngest musicians to play with the London Philharmonic and took the music world by storm with her album* The Violin Player.

Another band of the 1960s and '70s, Frank Zappa's Mothers of Invention, was used as a vehicle for band-audience involvement. Music was only a part of the performance, which also included satire and comedy. Anything could happen, from a bag of vegetables being opened and examined to "dead air", when the band stopped and completely ignored the audience. On one occasion, when the audience had become unsettled and angry, Zappa approached the microphone saying, "It brings out the hostilities in you, doesn't it?" Zappa went on to become a film producer and classical composer, and died in 1993.

There was a respite from "heavy metal" when in 1974 a breath of fresh air entered the pop charts with Abba. This Swedish quartet, who depended more on television and radio than live concerts to build an image, achieved their breakthrough by winning that year's Eurovision Song Contest with *Waterloo*, a song that became a top-ten hit in many countries and many languages.

Famous String Players

To play great music you must keep your eyes on a distant star.

The idea of a stringed instrument being a virtuoso instrument emerged during the Baroque period, when composers such as Arcangelo Corelli, who was a violinist, began to exploit the strings' expressiveness in *concerti grossi* and solo sonatas. Eighteenth-century refinements in stringed instrument design allowed for increasing technical brilliance by a number of great Italian virtuosi, culminating in the talents of the violinist Niccolò Paganini (1782–1840), who confirmed the star status of the soloist. He was also an expert on the mandolin, guitar and viola.

Violin

The great violinists of the Romantic period included Rudolphe Kreutzer (1766–1831), for whom Beethoven wrote his *Kreutzer Sonata*, and Joseph Joachim (1831–1907), to whom Brahms's Violin Concerto was dedicated. Fritz Kreisler (1875–1962) showed an early talent for the violin and by the time he was 15 had

ABOVE: Yehudi Menuhin was one of the most respected musicians who has ever lived. His violin-playing inspired young players.

ABOVE: David Oistrakh coupled the technical brilliance of Heifetz with the warmth of Menuhin. He can truly be said to be one of the greatest violinists of all time.

achieved worldwide success. His playing epitomized Viennese lilt and warmth, while his almost constant vibrato made him one of the founders of the modern school of violin-playing.

As well as being the foremost composer of his generation, Paul Hindemith (1895–1963) was also an outstanding viola player, playing in the Rebner and Amar Quartets, and the Opera Orchestra in Germany from 1915–23. Also an accomplished violinist, it was said he could play every instrument in the orchestra.

Yehudi Menuhin (1916–99) began his career as a child prodigy, and was at home in all types of music, achieving a unique tone and mastery of rhythm. He will always be remembered for his playing of the Elgar Violin Concerto under the direction of the composer, and as a humanitarian for the schools he founded for musically gifted children in England and Switzerland.

David Oistrakh (1908–74) achieved national recognition in the former Soviet Union after performing Glazunov's Violin Concerto in 1927. The Soviet authorities prevented him from performing outside the USSR until the early 1950s, but from then on he took the international stage by storm. He remained a Soviet citizen all his life and was committed to contemporary Russian composers such as Prokofiev and Shostakovich.

The Israeli violinist Itzhak Perlman (born 1945), although a victim of poliomyelitis at the age of four, was giving public recitals when he was ten years old. In his subsequent career, Perlman's charismatic stage presence, combined with his instinctive directness of musical expression, brilliant technique and a concern for refinement of detail, has brought him international recognition.

ABOVE: Mstislav Rostropovich was a close friend of Benjamin Britten, who wrote several cello works for him.

ABOVE: The charismatic Jacqueline du Pré made her debut at the age of 16.

Cello

As the cello took a more prominent role in chamber music during the 18th century, composers such as Liugi Boccherini (1743–1805) began to recognize its potential as a solo instrument. An early British virtuoso, Robert Lindley, began playing when he was five years old. His technique was said to be so brilliant that he was able to play first violin parts on his cello. In 1794, aged 18, Lindley played before the Prince Regent and, by 1826, had become lead cello with the Italian Opera in London.

Pablo Casals (1876–1973) probably did more for the cello than any other player. Although he is mainly remembered for his masterly playing of the Bach solo cello suites, Casals was also a conductor and a member of a chamber trio, and founded an annual festival of chamber music in France. Another influential cellist of the 20th century is Mstislav Rostropovich (born 1927), who has been immensely successful in playing the works of composers such as Shostakovich, Prokofiev and Britten.

The talent of Jacqueline du Pré (1945–87) was recognized at a very early age. She launched her professional career in 1961 with a concert at London's Wigmore Hall, at which she played a cello of 1672 by Antonio Stradivari. One of the great musical icons of the 20th century, she was admired by her audiences for the love she radiated in her playing, which was noted for its instinctive feeling for style as well as its technical proficiency. In 1973 her career was suddenly interrupted by the onset of multiple sclerosis, but she continued to teach.

Harp

Nicholas Bochsa (1789–1856), though a skilful player of almost every instrument, was best known for his expertise on the harp, an instrument on which he was constantly discovering new musical effects. Harpist to Louis XVIII, in 1817 he had to leave his native France hurriedly, due to his part-time business in forged documents. One of Bochsa's favourite pieces was his *Fantasia for Harp and Violin* which he often played with

ABOVE: Since making her London debut in 1963, Marisa Robles has become a professor at the Royal College of Music.

ABOVE: John Williams is a very versatile guitarist, playing classical, jazz and pop music – he founded the pop group, Sky.

Nicholas Mori, who was said to have handled his violin as tenderly as a mother her child, but as playfully as the child its toy.

The Spanish harpist Marisa Robles (born 1937) is one of the foremost players of the 20th century, noted for the quicksilver quality of her playing.

Lute and guitar

The eminent Spanish guitarist Andrés Segovia (1893–1987) was largely self-taught, but championed the guitar as a concert instrument, commissioning many new works. One of his pupils was Julian Bream (born 1933), who also took up the lute and quickly became a leading performer on it. In 1971, Bream began giving encouragement to guitar and lute makers by inaugurating the Semley Festival in Wiltshire to promote rare chamber music.

John Williams (born 1942) also studied guitar with Segovia. As a composer, he is particularly active in crossover projects, using tapes and electronics in his music and drawing on non-Western influences.

Famous Woodwind and Brass Players

*It takes perhaps a thousand poor musicians
to produce one virtuoso.*

RALPH VAUGHAN WILLIAMS (1872–1958)

As with other orchestral instruments, the expansion of the solo repertoire for woodwind and brass went hand in hand with technological advances that enabled the instruments to be played with far greater range and expressiveness.

Flute

Although Vivaldi and Mozart wrote for the solo flute, it was neglected during the 19th century, but found favour with French impressionists such as Debussy, and many modern composers have since written for it. The virtuoso James Galway (born 1939) is widely known as a popular soloist, but also spent many years as an orchestral player, including a period as principal flautist with the Berlin Philharmonic under Herbert von Karajan. A strong advocate of contemporary music, Galway's bright tone and twinkling

vibrato has brought him thousands of fans all around the world.

Jean-Pierre Rampal (born 1922) was an all-round musician of astonishing versatility. His repertoire ranged from Baroque to contemporary, while his playing was noted for its pure tone, subtle dynamics and exquisite phrasing.

Oboe

The sweet tone and expressive playing of Leon Goossens (1897–1988) set new standards for the instrument. Principal oboe with Henry Wood by the time he was 16, Goossens's phrasing, superlative finger technique and breath control were to influence many composers to write concertos for the oboe.

Another leading 20th-century oboist is the legendary Heinz Holliger (born 1939), who is an eminent exponent of sounding chords, double trills and

ABOVE: Leon Goossens was one of the finest oboe players of the 20th century. A member of a very musical family, he was brother to the conductor Eugene and the harpists Sidonie and Marie.

glissandos. He is not shy of experimentation; his work with sounds produced by a microphone placed within the bore of his instrument encouraged composers such as Hans Werner Henze to write for the oboe.

Clarinet

One of the 20th century's finest clarinettists was Benny Goodman (1909–86), a musician who was equally at home in classical music and jazz. He formed a 12-piece jazz band in 1934, but did not forsake his classical roots, for he later recorded the Mozart Clarinet Quintet with the Budapest Quartet, as well as commissioning works from Aaron Copland and Paul Hindemith.

ABOVE: One of Ireland's most popular musicians, James Galway has entertained millions with his flute-playing, performing both classical music and popular songs.

ABOVE: Barry Tuckwell studied horn technique with the virtuoso Dennis Brain (1921–57) on his arrival in England in 1950. He was Professor of Horn at the Royal Academy of Music (1963–74), launching his solo career in 1968.

Horn

Barry Tuckwell (born 1931) began his musical career in Melbourne, Australia, at the age of 15 and played with the Sydney Symphony Orchestra. He was principal horn with the London Symphony Orchestra from 1955 to 1968, in which year he founded the Tuckwell Wind Quintet. The leading horn player of his generation, Tuckwell is famed for his outstanding ability to make light of extreme technical and musical difficulties, achieving his marvellous tone by playing a large-bore Holton double horn, rather than the lighter-toned instrument preferred by many of his contemporaries.

Trumpet

One of the finest trumpet players was Louis Armstrong (1901–71), a man who almost single-handedly transformed jazz from a collective art to one of solo expression, exemplified in a series of 1920s recordings known as the "Hot Fives" and "Hot Sevens". His clear ringing trumpet sound

influenced many modern trumpet players, both jazz and classical.

The innovative player Maurice André (born 1933) has brought the trumpet to a whole new audience. One of his main contributions to trumpet-playing has been his pioneering of the small, four-valved piccolo trumpet. He has transcribed for it many Baroque compositions originally written for other wind instruments.

Another champion of modern trumpet music is Håkan Hardenberger (born 1961). He has had various works written specially for him, including Harrison Birtwistle's trumpet concerto *Endless Parade*. A master of musical effects, Hardenberger's playing combines technical brilliance with a great beauty of sound.

Wynton Marsalis (born 1961) comes from New Orleans, and is chiefly known as one of the most famous jazz trumpeters of his generation. However, such is his catholic taste that he is as much at home with Haydn's trumpet concertos as he is with the

ABOVE: Håkan Hardenberger is one of the world's top trumpet players, famous for his flawless technical ability and the beautiful quality of his tone.

ABOVE: The great jazz trumpeter Louis Armstrong in a scene from High Society.

Lincoln Center Jazz Orchestra. He is also a composer, and in 1997 won a Pulitzer Prize for his operatic piece *Blood on the Fields*.

Trombone

Many technical developments of the 20th century have been due to the influence of jazz musicians. One of the foremost jazz trombonists of the second half of the century is the German virtuoso Albert Mangelsdorff (born 1928). He played with various German jazz groups before forming his own band in 1958. In 1964, influenced by his recent tour of Asia, he started introducing eastern elements into his playing. His main claim to fame, however, is that he was the first trombonist to succeed in playing three and four-note chords on his instrument, a feat that he achieved by a skilful combination of lip and vocal sounds.

Famous Keyboard and Percussion Players

*The great pianists have nothing to show
save technique and affection.*

<small>LUDWIG VAN BEETHOVEN (1770–1827)</small>

The harpsichord had a major role in the Baroque ensemble as a continuo instrument, but other keyboard instruments, from majestic church organs to the domestic spinet, have largely been used as solo or accompanying instruments, or in chamber music. The modern piano is capable of suggesting the range and richness of an entire orchestra, and has a vast solo repertoire. It is sometimes used in modern orchestral music, but is treated like a special member of the percussion section.

Keyboard

One of the most remarkable keyboard players of the 18th century was William Crotch (1775–1847). Born in Norwich, the son of a carpenter, he was a child prodigy without parallel in the history of music. By the time he was two he was able to pick out tunes on an organ, and a year later his mother took him on a series of concert tours throughout England. As well as the piano Crotch also played the violin, which he did standing on a chair so as to be seen by his audience. In 1822 he was appointed principal of the newly established Royal Academy of Music.

Frédéric Chopin (1810–49) soon established himself as a pianist, making his public debut when he was eight years old. He arrived in Paris in 1831, where he was introduced to the artistic circle of Romantics such as Liszt, Berlioz and Bellini. Brought up on the

ABOVE: Clara Schumann, the wife of the composer Robert Schumann, was a fine performer and teacher and became one of the foremost pianists of the late 19th century.

music of Bach, Chopin was an intellectual who forged his own forms. His unique music is unmistakable, and he is recognized as one of the greatest composers for the piano.

Born in Hungary, Franz Liszt's (1811–86) early promise was rewarded by a subscription from five noblemen, which enabled him to study piano in Vienna. There he met Beethoven, who prophesied an excellent future for him. In 1831, on hearing Paganini's first concert in Paris, Liszt resolved there and then to become the Paganini of the piano. From 1838–47 he toured Europe, where the amazing strength of his fingers, which enabled him to execute the most rapid passages with amazing force, won him his reputation as the greatest piano virtuoso of his

ABOVE: Franz Liszt was the most popular pianist of his day. This caricature shows him being ecstatically received by his adoring female fans.

day. One of the outstanding musical personalities of the 19th century, Liszt created a brand new style that carried piano-playing technique further than ever before.

Clara Schumann (1819–96) was born in Leipzig, and was taught the piano by her father, the composer Friedrich Wieck, who also taught Robert Schumann. Clara made her musical debut in 1828, but after her marriage to Robert Schumann in 1840 she largely abandoned touring until after his death. Her playing was characterized by her seriousness and restraint, and her repertoire concentrated on Schumann, Beethoven, Chopin, Bach and Mozart. As well as editing many of her husband's works, she also composed many piano pieces of her own. She was also a famous and influential teacher.

The next generation of piano virtuosi included Ignacy Paderewski (1866–1941), who also became, briefly, prime minister of Poland in 1919; Sergei Rachmaninov (1873–1943), best known for his piano compositions in the Romantic style; and Artur Schnabel (1882–1951), an outstanding interpreter of Beethoven.

The Canadian pianist Glenn Gould (1932–82) performed on the concert

ABOVE: Evelyn Glennie, now a full-time solo percussionist, has collaborated with indigenous performers in many parts of the world to further audiences' understanding and appreciation of world music.

platform for only ten years, but was renowned for his charismatic recordings of the keyboard music of Bach. Alfred Brendel (born 1931) is known for his interpretations of Mozart, Beethoven, Schubert and Liszt. Vladimir Ashkenazy (born 1937), who was joint winner of the 1962 Tchaikovsky Piano Competition, was born in the former Soviet Union but left in 1963 and now lives in Iceland. A passionate pianist, he is equally known as a conductor.

Percussion

In Western music the percussionist has acquired virtuoso status in the 20th century, as composers have begun to use percussion more prominently and many new instruments from around the world have been added to the percussion section. The British player James Blades (1901–98) was a world-renowned orchestral player and an authority on percussion, who lectured and broadcast for many years. He influenced Evelyn Glennie (born 1965), who, although she partially lost her hearing at the age of eight,

was introduced to percussion when she was 12. Glennie made her solo debut at the Wigmore Hall in 1986. In 1989 she was the first solo percussionist to perform at the Proms. She has since toured with major orchestras and has had many pieces composed especially for her.

ABOVE: Russian-born Vladimir Ashkenazy shared first prize in the Tchaikovsky Piano Competition of 1962 with the British pianist John Ogdon (1937–89).

ABOVE: Although an infrequent piano performer, Mitsuko Uchida's inspired repertoire includes Mozart, Schoenberg, Birtwistle and Debussy.

Court Composers

*Music must be supported by the king and the princes,
for the maintenance of the arts is their duty.*

MARTIN LUTHER (1483–1546)

Before the 18th century, musicians and composers worked for princes and kings. Such was the prestige of top organists that Paul Hofhaimer (1459–1537), imperial organist to the Holy Roman Emperor Maximilian I, travelled with his royal master in his own special chariot. Maximilian's contemporary in England, Henry VIII, was also greatly interested in music and maintained a private band of 40 instrumentalists and singers.

Secular music was composed for private – not public – performance. Before 1750, professional musicians copied their music by hand, and even towards the end of the century Mozart often prevented his music from being widely circulated, as he feared it would be copied. As there was no protection of copyright or performing rights, patronage was the only way composers had of securing an income.

ABOVE: An autographed manuscript of Mozart's Symphony No. 8, written in brown ink on thick cream paper.

Lully

One of the most musically influential courts in Europe was that of Louis XIV (1643–1715). Jean-Baptiste Lully (1632–87) was born in Florence but had moved to France when he was 14, working first as a servant, then as a violinist. He entered royal service in 1652 and attained the post of Royal Composer in 1662. He developed the French operatic style, favouring short, simple songs rather than the florid arias so popular in Italy, and made a large fortune by obtaining a monopoly over French opera production.

Haydn

In 1761, Franz Joseph Haydn (1732–1809) entered the employment of the Hungarian Count Esterházy, with whom he spent the next 30 years. Although Esterházy's musical establishment was disbanded in 1790, Haydn retained his salary when he returned to Vienna. His long service with the family gave him great scope for composition, and he earned a reputation across Europe for his symphonies and string quartets, two forms for which he established the classical style. He then spent two years in London, where he wrote the last 12 of his 104 symphonies.

ABOVE: Lully went to Paris as a servant but his musical talents soon came to the attention of Louis XIV. He transformed music from a mere court pastime into a national art.

On his return to Vienna, he gave some lessons to a young German named Beethoven. Haydn was a prolific composer, and a humble and genial man who was well loved by the musicians he directed.

Bach

Orphaned at the age of ten, Johann Sebastian Bach (1685–1750) was brought up by his older brother, who taught him to play the organ, but his musical debut was as a choirboy at Lüneburg when he was 15. In 1703 he was appointed organist at Armstadt, but displeased his employers when he immersed himself in innovative organ music while neglecting his routine duties as choirmaster.

In 1708 he was appointed Kapellmeister to the Duke of Cöthen.

ABOVE: *Signed copy of the first movement of Bach's Sonata in G Minor for solo violin.*

ABOVE: *The one certain way for musicians to make a living in the 18th century was by having a royal patron: Mozart's father introduced his son to various European courts.*

As the Duke was a Calvinist, he required little music in his religious services, and Bach was able to concentrate on secular compositions and recitals. However, as a devout Lutheran, he wished to return to church music and in 1723 he accepted a more lowly post as cantor at the

Thomasschule in Leipzig, where he remained for the rest of his life.

Bach, who once said that it was his purpose to dispel sadness and bring joy, could turn his skills to almost any kind of music, although, in his own day, he received greater recognition as an organist than as a composer. His major standing as a composer was achieved only with the 19th-century revival of interest in his works.

Handel

George Frideric Handel (1685–1759) was born in Germany, but became a naturalized English citizen and one of England's greatest composers. Although he showed an early taste for music, Handel entered the University of Halle as a law student. However, after a short period as organist at the cathedral, he gave up his studies and went to Hamburg. It was here, in 1705, that his first operas *Almira* and *Nero* were produced. Five years later he became Kapellmeister to the Elector of Hanover. His period in Hanover was short, for by 1712 he was in London and in good favour with

Queen Anne, who gave him a life pension. In 1714 Anne died and his former master, the Elector, became King George I. Without doubt, Handel's greatest work is the *Messiah*, which he wrote in three weeks. It was first produced in Dublin in 1742, with a choir of about 30.

ABOVE: *In 17th-century England the main patron of music was the king. William III was no exception and encouraged his composers.*

ABOVE: *One of the most influential English composers of the first half of the 18th century was George Frideric Handel.*

Modern Composers

My music is best understood by children and animals.

IGOR STRAVINSKY (1882–1971)

While the Romantic composers of the 19th century believed that the prime function of music was to express emotion, those of the 20th century were more likely to see it as a search for new sounds and, consequently, new instruments on which to produce them.

United States

Aaron Copland (1900–90) used American jazz and folk idioms, as well as special effects, such as the orchestral reproduction of a gunfight in *Billy the Kid*. Other works by Copland that use folk music include *Rodeo* and *Appalachian Spring*. Another 20th-century American composer is Leroy Anderson (1908–75), whose light classical music gained wide popular appeal. His music was a blend of infectious melodies, popular dance rhythms and novel effects, such as the *pizzicato* strings in *Plink, Plank, Plonk*, the percussion in *The Syncopated Clock*, and unconventional "instruments" such as a typewriter and sandpaper.

John Cage (1912–92) was as much an inventor as a composer. A pupil of Schoenberg, Cage relegated harmony and pitch to a secondary role and gave priority to rhythm and noise. He drew up large charts on which he plotted rhythmic structures to compose works such as his *Concerto for Prepared Piano*. In *Music of Changes* the progressions all depend on the tossing of a coin.

Russia

Dimitri Shostakovich (1906–75) graduated from Petrograd Conservatory in 1925. His First

ABOVE: *Although Shostakovich ran foul of the Russian state in 1948, he was politically rehabilitated in 1956 and his work greatly influenced young Russian composers.*

Symphony, composed while he was still a student, won international acclaim in 1926, but his Fourth was withdrawn in 1936 during rehearsal when the Stalinist authorities objected to his opera, *Lady Macbeth of the Mtsensk District*. Although he attempted to ingratiate himself with his Fifth Symphony, his relationship with the government remained uneasy, and in 1948 he was denounced for "formalism" and fired from his teaching post at the Leningrad Conservatory. He undertook to bring his work nearer to "folk art", and finally regained his job in 1960.

Shostakovich wrote 15 symphonies and several operas and ballets, as well as chamber, choral and piano music, and his work had a great influence on younger Russian composers.

ABOVE: *Aaron Copland's use of the jazz and folk idioms of his native land in his music cannot fail to stir up images of the America of the late 19th and early 20th centuries.*

ABOVE: In his youth Messiaen used to write down birdsong, which he included in his music. Taken prisoner by the Germans in World War II, his Quartet for the End of Time *was written in a concentration camp.*

France

Paul Dukas (1865–1935) achieved worldwide success for his orchestral work of 1897, *L'Apprenti sorcier* and, although he wrote some successful music for the stage, it is virtually by this work alone that Dukas is remembered. His severe self-criticism reached such a pitch that he refused to publish any new composition, eventually going as far as to burn everything not yet published. His surviving work includes the opera *Ariane et Barbe-bleue* (1907), *La Péri*, a ballet published in 1912, and a sonata for the piano in E minor.

One of Dukas's pupils at the Paris Conservatoire was Olivier Messiaen (1908–92). Messiaen, an organist as well as a composer, was greatly influenced by Indian and eastern music, and his orchestral compositions display great rhythmic complexity.

Electronic music

The *ondes Martenot* ("Martenot waves"), one of the earliest successful electronic instruments, was patented by the French cellist and radio engineer, Maurice Martenot (1896–1980) in 1928. Using oscillating valves as the sound source, the pitch was controlled by moving one hand along a wire, while the other hand operated a number of "expression" keys. Later a keyboard was added for pitch orientation. The *ondes Martenot* was first used in an orchestra for a performance of Messiaen's *Turangalíla* Symphony in 1947. Arthur Honegger (1892–1955) and Pierre Boulez also wrote music for the instrument.

In 1949 an electronic music studio was set up in Paris to further the work of Pierre Schaeffer (born 1910), a radio technician and the founder of *musique concrète*, a term he coined to describe a form in which pre-existing real sounds were manipulated in various ways and combined into a kind of sound collage. Other composers to use the studio included Stockhausen, Messiaen and Boulez.

Jean-Michel Jarre (born 1948) became a pupil of Schaeffer in 1968. He combines electronic music with melodic orchestration to produce commercially successful recordings such as *Oxygène* (1977) and *Equinoxe* (1978). He has mounted a series of live performances on a huge scale, culminating in a Bastille Day celebration in Paris in 1990 that was attended by 2.5 million people.

ABOVE: Boulez is a great exponent of avant-garde music. He once said that his music, like fashion, was self-destructive so that it could be replaced by a new collection.

ABOVE: Jean-Michel Jarre studied counterpoint, fugue and harmony at the Paris Conservatoire and released his first electro-acoustic recording, La Cage, *in 1969.*

Role of the Conductor

It is better to conduct with the ear than with the arm.
The rest follows automatically.

GEORG SOLTI (1912–97)

Although the role of the virtuoso conductor was a 19th-century phenomenon, there had always been one member of an ensemble whose duty it was to direct the others and so ensure a uniformity of performance. In ancient Greece the "giver of time beat with his stave up and down", while in Rome, time was indicated by the leader stamping his feet. In 17th-century France it was the custom to beat time loudly on the floor with a large staff – which on one occasion had fatal consequences. In 1687, while conducting a *Te Deum* to celebrate the king's recovery from sickness, Jean-Baptiste Lully brought his long staff down on his foot instead of the floor and died of the subsequent gangrene poisoning. The staff survives today both as the conductor's baton and in the mace carried by drum majors

leading military bands. During the 15th and 16th centuries some choral conductors kept time by waving a rolled-up sheet of music.

Until the 18th century it was usual for the conductor to be the composer. He generally directed the band from his seat at the harpsichord, although in France it bcame fashionable for the first violin to direct. This was also the case with the Mannheim orchestra, an ensemble that was greatly influenced by French practice.

Although Beethoven is known to have conducted his own works, his methods were far from conventional. When conducting from the piano, he bent lower to indicate that he wanted the music played softly. When the music came to a *crescendo*, he raised

LEFT: The modern conductor's baton — used for beating time and indicating expression — is a thin tapering stick about 50cm/20in long. Although first seen in the late 18th century, batons did not come into general use until the 1820s.

himself by degrees and, upon the commencement of the *forte*, would spring bolt upright. To increase the *forte* even more, he would often join in with a shout to the orchestra.

From the late 18th century music became more complex, with each instrumental section having more solo music to play. Although Carl Maria von Weber (1786–1826) conducted an orchestra with a baton in 1817, the first man to conduct an orchestra in the modern sense – moving his hands and arms without making a sound himself – was the German violinist Louis Spohr (1784–1859), leader of the orchestra of the Theater an der Wien, who conducted the Philharmonic Society of London in 1820.

In Vienna, the directors of the new waltz orchestras of the early 19th century, such as Johann Strauss the Elder (1804–49) and his rival Joseph Lanner (1801–43), led while playing the violin, beating time with the bow. This custom is sometimes resurrected by the conductors at the annual New Year's concert in Vienna.

Nineteenth-century conductors took on more and more responsibility for the performance. They established the speed and helped players come in at the right time. They decided how the

ABOVE: After making his conducting debut in 1943 with the New York Philharmonic, Leonard Bernstein (1918–90) conducted many famous orchestras, including La Scala, the Vienna Philharmonic, the Israel Philharmonic and the London Symphony Orchestra.

ABOVE: The custom in the 18th century was for the leader of a musical band to conduct from the keyboard. Here Bach is seen conducting an ensemble from the clavichord.

music should be played and phrased. They were also more necessary because orchestras were growing larger. Although he never achieved his dream, Berlioz's ideal orchestra size was 465. Conducting soon came to be regarded as an important profession in its own right and, as the 19th century progessed, a conductor cult grew. It became usual for composers to conduct not just their own works but also those of others.

In opera it was customary for the conductor to concentrate on the singers rather than the band, and to this end he was placed immediately in front of – and facing – the stage, with the orchestra behind him, following his beat as best they could. It was not until 1897, when Gustav Mahler (1860–1911) became conductor of the Vienna State Opera, that the podium was moved to the back of the orchestra pit.

ABOVE: Some conductors use very subtle gestures, in which even minor movements of the forearm can cause the players to respond instantly.

Conducting with style

ABOVE AND LEFT: Many conductors are showmen, relishing their position in the limelight, and their antics sometimes seem intended more to impress the audience than direct the orchestra. These photographs show just a few of the hundreds of gestures and instructions made by a conductor within the context of a performance.

Famous Conductors

*You must have the score in your head,
not your head in the score.*

HANS VON BÜLOW (1830–94)

In his *Notes for Conductors*, Richard Strauss advises a conductor to put his left thumb in the armpit of his waistcoat and lead the orchestra with the right. It is, so Strauss advises, the audience and not the conductor who should sweat. One man who followed Strauss's advice to the extreme was Arthur Nikisch (1855–1922), who certainly allowed the baton to do all the work. He never distracted the orchestra or the audience with elaborate gestures, and conducted almost solely from the wrist down. Indeed, any minor movement of his forearm would so alarm the players that they would instantly respond with a massive *fortissimo*. Amongst Nikisch's disciples were Fritz Reiner (1888–1963) and Adrian Boult (1889–1983).

ABOVE: Arthur Nikisch, seen here with the Berlin Philharmonic Orchestra, was known for conducting the orchestra in a subtle manner, moving his arms only slightly.

ABOVE: The English conductor Sir Thomas Beecham founded the London Philharmonic Orchestra in 1932. He was especially known for his interpretations of Delius's music.

Thomas Beecham (1879–1961) never had a technique! His baton did whatever the state of the performance prompted. He disdained to be seen beating anything less complex than phrases, but at the same time he discreetly beat time by opening and closing the fingers of his left hand. He was renowned for his dry wit: during one rehearsal he remarked that the second trumpet was too loud. The embarrassed leader had to explain that the second trumpet player had telephoned to say that he would be

a little late. Unperturbed, Sir Thomas replied: "Well, when he comes, tell him he is too loud."

The qualities of a conductor as a personality are always important. That some have more pleasant personalities than others is a fact of life, and some, however musical they are, leave a lot to be desired. Arturo Toscanini (1867–1957) was notoriously temperamental. At one rehearsal of Verdi's opera *Falstaff*, he threw the score at four different women soloists, alleging that they had not learnt their parts. At another rehearsal he threw his gold watch to the floor and stamped on it. His disregard for other people's feelings was legendary and on one occasion, when a red carpet was laid from the stage entrance to the podium as a mark of respect for him, Toscanini refused to enter until it was taken up, growling "*Non sono un cardinale.*"

Most great conductors have, however, been more amenable and well respected by the musicians with whom they work. The British conductor John Barbirolli (1899–1970), who succeeded Toscanini as conductor of the New York Philharmonic in 1937, was vivacious and charming. He returned to Britain in 1943 to become permanent conductor of the Hallé Orchestra in Manchester. Another well-loved figure was Malcolm Sargent (1895–1967). Particularly noted for his choral work, from 1928 he was the conductor of the Royal Choral Society. Sargent was noted not only for his

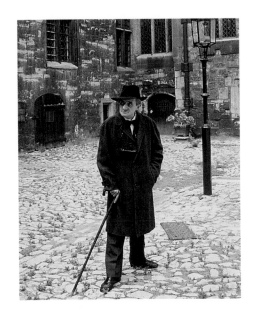

ABOVE: The son of an émigré Italian violinist, Barbirolli became one of Britain's foremost conductors. For his services to music, he was knighted in 1949.

immediate grasp of a complicated score and for his extraordinarily effective "stick technique", but also as a "showman". In 1950 he succeeded Adrian Boult as conductor of the BBC Symphony Orchestra. Sargent, the natural successor to Henry Wood as principal conductor of the Promenade Concerts, was equally at home with classical and modern music, and many young and inexperienced players gained much confidence by his support.

Herbert von Karajan (1908–89) was a far less accessible man and personified the image of the conductor as star. Between the 1950s and '70s he was the dominant figure in European music. While presiding over the Berlin Philharmonic for 35 years, his influence also spread over the Vienna State Opera, the Salzburg Festival, the Vienna Symphony Orchestra, the Philharmonia Orchestra in London and La Scala in Milan. Karajan was an

imperious, stubborn and demanding conductor who worked only on his own terms. Throughout his career he continued to question and rework his own musical interpretations, but his intimate knowledge of the players of the Berlin Philharmonic and his belief in their potential enabled him to turn it into one of the world's finest orchestras.

His predecessor in Berlin had been Wilhelm Furtwängler (1886–1954), whose conducting was characterized by a curious wavering beat that often confused those who were not used to him. He was particularly associated with the music of Wagner, at a time when it came to stand for the ideals of the Nazi regime in Germany. Otto Klemperer (1885–1973), on the other hand, was denounced by the Nazis and left Germany to become an American citizen. Another leading conductor of his time, his performances were notable for their attention to detail, especially in the woodwind section.

An outstanding figure of the new generation is Simon Rattle (born 1955). At the age of 16 he took lessons in conducting from Pierre Boulez, and in 1974 won first prize in the Bournemouth International Conducting Competition. In the same

ABOVE: In 1980 the British conductor Sir Simon Rattle was appointed principal conductor of the City of Birmingham Orchestra, which he transformed into a world-class ensemble. He has a deep solidarity with his orchestras.

year he was appointed assistant conductor of the Bournemouth Symphony Orchestra. In 1980 he became principal conductor of the City of Birmingham Symphony Orchestra, which he transformed into a world-class ensemble. In 1999 it was announced that he would replace Claudio Abbado as chief conductor of the Berlin Philharmonic in 2002.

ABOVE: Herbert von Karajan was one of the most respected conductors of the 20th century. He was principal conductor of the Berlin Philharmonic for 35 years.

ABOVE: Sir Georg Solti studied under notables such as Bartók and Kodály, and was Musical Director of the Chicago Symphony Orchestra until his death in 1997.

Famous Concert Halls and Orchestras

...For we must have music, We must have music
To drive our fears away.

NOEL COWARD (1899–1973)

Until the 18th century, public concerts as they are known today did not exist. One of the first rooms to be devoted to formal concerts was that opened in London by Thomas Hickford in 1711. From then on other custom-built concert halls and opera houses gradually started to appear all over Europe.

German patrons of music built concert halls on a grand scale. At Schwetzingen, the Elector of Palatine built a new opera house capable of holding an audience of 5000, while Duke Karl Theodor of Württemberg bankrupted his entire principality to provide sensational opera productions at Mannheim.

The Berlin Opera House was built by Frederick the Great of Prussia (1740–86). A notable flautist and patron of music, Frederick was deeply immersed in French culture and maintained a French-speaking court. Opened in 1773, the Opera House, which employed singers from Italy and dancers from France, was equipped with parking space for 1000 carriages. The staircases were so wide that sedan

ABOVE: *This painting by Ludwig Edward Lutke shows the German State Opera House in Berlin, c.1845.*

ABOVE: *The Amsterdam Concertgebouw Orchestra was founded in 1888. Its hall is renowned for its magnificent acoustics.*

chairs could be carried up to the fourth tier of the boxes, and three enormous chandeliers illuminated the whole auditorium.

In London, purpose-built concert halls included Carlisle House, Soho Square (1764); the Pantheon, Oxford Street (1772); and the Hanover Square Rooms (1775). Halls were also opened in some major provincial centres, such as Bath, which, thanks to its spa, was the centre of English fashionable society in the 18th century.

Throughout the 19th century the orchestras involved in London concerts contained so many of the same players that it would be difficult to describe each orchestra as different. Players had little or no

financial security and were engaged for each concert, not for the entire season. The custom of sending a deputy to the rehearsals, or even the concert, had become established, meaning that the composition of the orchestra was constantly changing.

One of the first conductors to recruit musicians for an entire season was Charles Hallé (1819–95). Hallé had made his reputation in Paris, but was driven to England by the revolution of 1848 and eventually settled in Manchester, which had an influential German community. He threw himself heartily into the town's musical life and in 1857 founded what was to become the celebrated Hallé

ABOVE: *The New York Metropolitan Opera House was founded in 1883 but was rebuilt after a fire destroyed the original building.*

Orchestra. Its members were always present at both rehearsal and concert, making the orchestra the most disciplined and efficient band in the country. They never sounded, as did so many other orchestras, like a bunch of instrumentalists thrown together for a single event.

During the 20th century several great orchestras have been founded in London, including the London Philharmonic, which was founded in

ABOVE: Musical events held at the Royal Albert Hall in London range from brass band contests to rock concerts.

1932 by Thomas Beecham, and the BBC Symphony Orchestra, which was founded in 1930 and was the first orchestra to offer an annual salary and paid holidays.

As the 20th century progressed, orchestras faced the problem of financial support. The Boston Symphony Orchestra was founded in 1881 by the financier Henry Lee Higginson. He gave his conductors absolute artistic freedom and kept the orchestra at the highest level of achievement. Its financial future was assured by Higginson's creation of a body of 300 guarantors. Further south, the New York Philharmonic was founded in 1842. For the first 66 years of its existence it was run by an internal committee of musicians.

However, in 1908, due to financial difficulties, the orchestra was taken over by a syndicate.

The Berlin Philharmonic Orchestra, which acquired its high international reputation under the directorship of Herbert von Karajan, is funded by the city of Berlin, and has its home in an acoustically brilliant concert hall affectionately known as the "circus tent". Although it has a capacity of 2000, the seats virtually surround the orchestra, giving the hall a feeling of intimacy.

The audience at the Royal Albert Hall in London is seated in a vast ellipse, but had to suffer poor acoustics until they were remedied in the 1960s. The brick and glass building was built from 1867–71, and is universally known as the venue for the annual Henry Wood Promenade Concerts, which have been performed there since World War II when their former home, the Queen's Hall, was destroyed.

The Sydney Opera House on Bennelong Point is one of the city's most notable features. Designed by

ABOVE: Kurt Masur conducting the New York Philharmonic Orchestra in 1999. Masur made his United States debut in 1974.

Jørn Utsen, the building was largely financed by the Australian lottery and was opened in 1973. Its programme offers 16 different operas a year and there is a performance almost every night during the winter.

The world's largest opera house is the Metropolitan Opera House at the Lincoln Center in New York, completed in 1966 with an audience capacity of 4065.

ABOVE: Looking like something that has just emerged from the sea, the main features of the Sydney Opera House in Australia are its nine flying roofs, the highest point of which is 67m/220ft above sea level.

Acoustics: the science of sound.

Air: a simple tune for instrument or voice.

Aleatoric music: music in which random elements can determine the course of the piece.

Aria: an operatic solo.

Atonal: having no definite key centre or tonality.

Baroque: the musical period from about 1600–1750. From the Portuguese *barrôco*, meaning "irregular pearl".

Basso continuo: an accompanying bass line written in "shorthand".

Bell: the flared or bulbous end of many aerophones.

Blues: a slow, sad musical idiom characterized by the fusion of African and European music.

Chamber music: includes solo vocal music, music written for a single instrument or a small group of instruments, all parts being equal in importance.

Chamber orchestra: a small-sized orchestra, originally playing in a room or small hall.

Chord: the effect that is produced by sounding two or more notes together.

Chorus: a choir, which can consist of mixed voices, male voices or female voices.

Chromatic scale: the European 12-note scale of semitones.

Coll'arco: direction to play strings with the bow.

Compass: the range of a voice or instrument.

Concert pitch: the standard of pitch to which instruments are usually tuned. At present the A above middle C (*a'*) is set at 440 Hertz.

Concerto: a composition for one or more solo instruments and orchestra.

Consort: a group of instruments of the same family.

Coquille: the hole through a valve that allows the passage of air from one side to the other.

Counterpoint: the weaving of two or more melodic lines together so that they harmonize with each other.

Course: two or three strings lying close together, sounded together and tuned to either unison or octave pitch.

Court composer: a musician employed as a royal composer.

Crescendo: gradually increasing in loudness.

Diatonic scale: any one of the major or minor scales of five tones and two semitones.

Diminuendo: gradually decreasing in loudness.

Drone: a pipe or string that sounds a sustained tone.

Dynamics: variations in loudness and softness.

Folk music: music and dances of unknown authorship passed orally through the generations.

Frog: the part of the bow that tightens the hair.

Glissando: a slide up or down, played, for example, by sweeping across harp strings or sliding the finger along a violin string.

Gregorian chant: solo and unison plainsong choral chants associated with Pope Gregory I.

Harmonics: the fundamental and overtones of a given tone.

Harmony: the simultaneous sounding of combined notes.

Idiophone: an instrument made of naturally sonorous materials, not needing any additional tension as do strings and drumskins.

Jack: a thin strip of wood that carries the plectrum in plucked keyboard instruments.

Janissary music: a style of percussive military music, influenced by Turkish music, popular in 18th-century Europe.

Jazz: a type of "ragtime" music which developed in the southern states of America in the late 19th century, coming into prominence in New Orleans at the turn of the century.

Libretto: the text of an opera.

Madrigal: a polyphonic composition for voices.

Melody: a succession of notes, varying in pitch, which have an organized and recognizable pattern.

Microtone: any interval smaller than a semitone.

Neumes: a system of musical notation dating from the 7th to the 14th centuries. Beginning as an approximation of the shape of the melody, the system developed into precise indications of pitch used in church plainsong manuals.

Opera: a drama set to music, sung by singers in costume with instrumental accompaniment.

Orchestra: originally a place where the Greek chorus sang and danced. The term now refers to a mixed body of instrumentalists for the performance of symphonic and other works.

Ornamentation: the insertion of a note or notes additional to the main tune, for decoration. Examples include trills and mordents.

Overblowing: the production of overtones on a wind instrument.

Pegs: tuning pins used on a stringed instrument.

Pitch: the "height" or "depth" of a note, determined by the frequency of vibrations producing it.

Pizzicato: direction to pluck strings with the fingers.

Plainsong: traditional ritual vocal melodies of the Western Christian church sung in free rhythm, culminating in Gregorian chant in 1st-century Rome.

Plectrum: a device used for plucking strings.

Polyphony: music with several interwoven melodic lines.

Polytonality: simultaneous use of several keys.

Rhythm: that which pertains to the time aspect of music (as opposed to the pitch), including the effect of beats, accents, measures, and the grouping of beats into measures and phrases.

Score: written or printed ensemble music with all the parts set out one above the other on the page.

Soundboard: the flat front of the body of a chordophone that receives the vibrations from the strings and reflects them.

Symphony: a large-scale orchestral composition, usually in four movements.

Tonic: keynote of the diatonic scale.

Transposition: the translation of a piece of music into a key other than that in which it was originally written.

Troubadour: a travelling French musician of the 14th century. The equivalent peripatetic musicians in Germany were called *Minnesinger* and in England they were known as minstrels.

Turmmusik: music played from a 16th-century German church or town-hall tower, usually using instruments such as cornetts, trombones and trumpets, in four or five-part harmony.

Acknowledgements

The publisher would like to thank the following picture libraries for the use of their pictures in the book (l=left, r=right, t=top, b=bottom, u=upper, m=middle). Every effort has been made to acknowledge the pictures properly, however we apologize if there are any unintentional omissions which will be corrected in future editions.

AKG, London: 14t, bl, br; 15t; 16t, b; 17tl, bl, br; 21br; 30bl; 36bl; 38t, br; 43t; 45bl, br; 47bl; 49tl; 54r; 60t; 63b; 66t, b; 78bl; 81tr; 83bl; 86l, r; 89tl.

Arena Images Ltd: 6tr; 32t; 34br; 35tr, br; 36br; 37bl; 39tr; 50b; 55b; 81tl.

Art Archive Ltd: 6bl; 7b; 8–9; 10br; 15m; 18l, r; 19t, bl; 22t; 25b; 27l; 42r; 46b; 47t; 55tl; 59t, b; 67m, b.

Bridgeman Art Library, London: 12t; 20tl; 21tl; 28t; 31tl, tr; 43b; 56t; 57t; 61tr; 62t; 74bl; 92bl; *Index* 12bl; 30bl; 54l; *Peter Willi* 7t.

Camera Press Ltd: 15br; 31br; 58t, b, (all flags); 59 (all flags); 61bl, br; 63tl; 71tr; 72t; 74t; 75tl; 76l, r; 77bl; 80l; 83t; 84l; 93tl, b.

Christie's Images: 21bl.

Frank Lane Picture Agency Limited: *Roger Wilmshurst* 10t.

gettyone Stone: 21tr; 22br;

29t (3rd from left); 61tl; 68bl, br; 69t; 72b.

Hutchinson Library: 12bl, br; 13t, b; 23t.

Lebrecht Collection, London: 11t; 20tr; 22bl; 24l, r; 25tl; 26t, bl, br; 30t; 33tl; 42l; 45t; 46t; 48t, b; 49m, b; 56b; 60b; 62b; 64b; 67t; 69br; 74br; 82l, r; 85tl, br; 89tr; 90l; 92br; *Zdenek Chrapek* 56m; *N. Dyson* 68t; *Mike Evans* 51t; *David Farrell* 55tr; 79b; 91tl; *Betty Freeman* 87m; *Richard Haughton* 57b; *C. R. Henderson* 65t; *S. Lauterwasser* 49tr; 78t; 88b; 91bl; *Suzie Maeder* 83br; 87t; *Morris* 69bl; *Kate Mount* 51t; 53m; *Odile Noel* 50t; 65b; *F. Noronha* 36t; *Pictorial Press* 63tr; 73tr, b; 75bl; 77br; *Wladimir Polak* 91tr; 91br; *Private Collection* 47br; *Royal Academy of Music* 80r; *G. Salter* 32br; 52t, b; 64t; *Chris Stock* 13m; 92t; *Toby Wales* 93tr.

Mary Evans Picture Library: 6br; 11m, b; 15bl; 17tr; 19br; 25tr; 27r; 28br; 31bl; 34t; 44; 84r; 85tr, bl.

Performing Arts Library: 70t; 90r; *Clive Barda* 53t, b; 57m; 63m; 78br; *Sisi Burn* 81b; *Fritz Curzon* 33b; *Linda Rich* 20b.

Redferns Music Picture Library: 35tr; 51b; 70bl, br; 71tl, b; 73tl; 75tr, br; 77tl, tr; 79tl, tr; 87b; 89b (all in panel).

Simon Broughton: 23bl, br.

Index